The Really Useful
Creativity Book

What is creativity and how do we teach it?

The Really Useful Creativity Book provides approaches and ideas that will enable children to develop their creativity. Written for the primary school teacher, student or trainee teacher, the book shows you how creativity can flourish in your classroom.

With examples of practice included throughout, the issues covered include:

- Everyday creativity: ideas to get started on straight away
- Planning: with ideas for cross-curricular planning, and many other ways to plan for creativity
- Creativity and the environment: starting with the classroom and school, then going further afield
- Creative partnerships: working with other people to stimulate children's creativity
- The drama of creativity: showing how teachers – and children – can adopt 'the Mantle of the Expert'
- Thinking about creativity: thinking skills for your children, and ways of thinking for you.

This lively, stimulating book will help busy teachers working with the National Curriculum to develop children's creativity.

Dominic Wyse is a senior lecturer in early years and primary education at the University of Cambridge, UK.

Pam Dowson is a teacher and Assistant Director of Learning in a First School and contributes to English courses at the University of Cambridge, UK.

The Really Useful Series

The Really Useful Maths Book: A Guide for Primary Teachers
Tony Brown & Henry Liebling

The Really Useful Science Book: A Framework of Knowledge for Primary Teachers, 3rd Edition
Steve Farrow

The Really Useful Literacy Book: Being Creative with Literacy in the Primary Classroom, 2nd Edition
Tony Martin, Chira Lovat & Glynis Purnell

The Really Useful ICT Book: A Framework of Knowledge for Primary Teachers
Nick Packard & Steve Higgins

The Really Useful Book of ICT in the Early Years
Harriet Price (forthcoming)

The Really Useful Creativity Book

Dominic Wyse and Pam Dowson

Routledge
Taylor & Francis Group

LONDON AND NEW YORK

First published 2009
by Routledge
2 Park Square, Milton Park, Abingdon, Oxon OX14 4RN

Simultaneously published in the USA and Canada
by Routledge
270 Madison Ave, New York, NY 10016

Routledge is an imprint of the Taylor & Francis Group, an informa business

© 2009 Dominic Wyse and Pam Dowson

Typeset in Palatino by
Keystroke, 28 High Street, Tettenhall, Wolverhampton
Printed and bound in Great Britain by
CPI Antony Rowe, Chippenham, Wiltshire

British Library Cataloguing in Publication Data
A catalogue record for this book is available from the British Library

Library of Congress Cataloging in Publication Data
Wyse, Dominic, 1964–
    The really useful creativity book/Dominic Wyse and Pam Dowson.
        p. cm.
        Includes bibliographical references and index.
    1. Creative ability—Study and teaching (Primary)   I. Dowson, Pam
(Pamela Joan), 1950–   II. Title.
    BF408.W97 2008
    372.5–dc22   2008016968

ISBN10: 0–415–45696–7 (pbk)
ISBN13: 978–0–415–45696–8 (pbk)

Dominic dedicates this book to Pascal Wyse, a very creative and wonderful person.

Pam dedicates this book to Romy Craig – her best creation.

Contents

Figures

Tables

Boxes

Acknowledgements

Our heartfelt thanks to Anna Clarkson for her inspiration for the book and for starting the series in the first place; to Lucy Wainwright for keeping us on the straight and narrow; and to Stephanie Thwaites for her brilliant work supporting many projects.

Particular thanks to David Spendlove for his tireless enthusiasm and curiosity, and for his collaboration over the creativity research.

Finally, thanks to the past and present pupils and staff of St Mary's CEVAP School, Mildenhall, for their willingness to take on challenges and move learning forward.

Introduction

This book began its life with a blank sheet of paper. The paper was to be filled with ideas.

We are tempted to say that these two sentences are so far from reality that they are lies! But we are being somewhat unfair to ourselves. It is true that before we started the book there were, metaphorically speaking, just blank sheets of paper. It is also true to say that in order to create the book, the paper had to be filled with ideas. However, the reality of the process involved many influences that are not conveyed by the metaphor. First of all, Anna Clarkson, who commissioned the book for the publisher, enticed us to add a book on creativity to the Really Useful series. Then Dominic spoke to Pam about the project. They had been working together because Pam was seconded from her job as a classroom teacher to the Faculty of Education at the University of Cambridge for one day a week. Together they discussed the kind of book they wanted to write. Meetings were held and a book proposal emerged. Referees who read the proposal made suggestions. Then the writing began. But did the writing follow the plan so clearly expressed in the proposal? To a large degree yes, but the process of writing also inspired changes along the way.

Our different experiences helped us to fashion the writing. Dominic's interest in creativity began with his experience as a musician. Once he became a teacher, the creativity that is a part of music fed into a growing interest in the teaching and learning of English. His first book, *Primary Writing*, had children's choices and a belief in their imagination at the heart of its account of the process approach to teaching writing. Later he collaborated with Russell Jones on another book, *Creativity in the Primary Curriculum*. Pam's interest in creativity came from her belief that a holistic approach to teaching and learning is vital. She was able to develop these ideas in the context of a school that embraces creativity. We share something of the commissioning, planning and the writing process with you because this all contributed to what was a creative act – an act that was influenced by many things; an act that required disciplined thinking; and an act that finally resulted in something new.

The creativity field has frequently been dominated by two key questions: (1) How do we define creativity; and (2) How do we teach creativity? The first chapter of the book offers our definition of creativity. It is worth stating here:

> **Creativity** – a person's capacity to produce new or original ideas, insights, restructurings, inventions, or artistic objects, which are accepted by suitably qualified people as being of scientific, aesthetic, social, or technological value.

To see how we arrived at the definition and whose work we drew upon, you will need to read Chapter 1. We hope we have produced some new insights in the writing of this book. We will leave you as the qualified people to decide!

You will find some ideas in the book that you are familiar with. The key thing as far as we are concerned is not that the idea may be familiar, but the new way it could be used to foster creativity. In other words, when the ideas, strategies, activities and ways of working that we promote are used in the classroom, can you find/see/hear/intuit your pupils' capacity to produce the new or original?

If the first chapter explains what we mean by creativity (and creative teaching, and creative learning), then the other chapters in the book suggest how we teach in ways that foster creativity. There is nothing easy about creativity, although the spontaneous way that children create things may somethimes lead us to think that there is. Creativity is made possible by disciplined thinking. As a professional, the first thing you have to do is organise your teaching for creativity. This may require you to think in a completely different way about everything, including the National Curriculum (however, we do give you a gentle introduction by suggesting quick changes to practice in the chapter called 'Everyday creativity').

If the environment of your classroom is important, then so are other environments. We help you see how the local environment of the school and the wider environment of the community, the nation and even the world are resources for creativity! You will not be alone in your mission, though: partnerships can be a tremendous boost to creativity. Perhaps the most challenging practice featured in the book is where you and the children put on 'the Mantle of the Expert'. Once you recover from the exhilaration of this, the chapter that follows suggests a pause to think – about thinking. The final chapter offers a challenge: can the primary curriculum be *fundamentally* a creative one, from top to bottom?

To conclude this introduction, then, here are three thoughts to stimulate your creative capacity:

- Creativity is a right, not a privilege;
- Nobody can be creative without control;
- Creativity is not magic, but it can be magical.

1 Defining creativity

When you think about the word 'creativity', what thoughts does it spark? Perhaps famous creative people such as Picasso, Einstein or Mozart. Maybe you see creativity as particularly related to the work of composers, writers and artists. You may feel that creativity is something that only some talented people have, or that it is something that we all have. Maybe you see an important role for creativity in areas like business, innovation and enterprise. Even in the first few sentences of this book, we have covered a wide range of concepts that arguably are part of what creativity is. However, for a book that is all about creativity, if possible we need to establish a definition. Here's the one from the *Oxford English Dictionary* (OED): 'Creative power or faculty; ability to create'. This definition begs the question, how do we define *creative*? When 'creative' is used as an adjective, the first definition from the OED is 'Having the quality of creating, given to creating; of or pertaining to creation; originative', which naturally is closely linked to the definition for 'creativity'. When 'creative' is used as a noun, one of the definitions states that a 'creative' is a person whose job involves creative work. Another noun definition refers rather technically to creative material produced for advertising campaigns – for example, 'the creative was designed by agency Saatchi and Saatchi'. 'Creative' in this context refers to the materials used.

The 'ability to create', which is part of the definition of creativity, is a seemingly straightforward and attractive idea for our purposes. Anybody can create something, therefore everybody can be creative: creativity is a human ability. But what is this ability like and how is it demonstrated? To answer these questions, we need to move away from dictionary definitions to more extended scholarly work on the subject.

Creativity research

A significant amount of influential research on creativity has come from the United States. The modern age of creativity research in America began with Guilford's presidential address to the American Psychological Association in 1950. Guilford began by making a close link between abilities and creative people, something he also described as a series of character traits. He described the neglect of the study of creativity as 'appalling' (1987, p. 34). Guilford noted the importance of creative talent to industry, science, engineering and government. A key feature of his presentation was that creativity can be expected, 'however feeble, of almost all individuals' (ibid., p. 36). Research through the 1970s and 1980s was largely concerned with more detailed attempts to define and, ultimately, measure creativity. The Torrance tests of creativity were one of the best-known examples of such measurement. Feldman and Benjamin (2006) locate this work in the tradition of psychometric assessment and point out that the frequently cited ideas of 'technological inventiveness' and 'ideational fluency' emerged from this strand of research.

One definition that has proved to be influential was established by Vernon (1989, p. 94): 'Creativity means a person's capacity to produce new or original ideas, insights, restructurings, inventions, or artistic objects, which are accepted by experts as being of scientific, aesthetic, social, or technological value.' The idea that creativity requires originality is important. However, originality does not exist in a vacuum; it is inspired by the field of thought that has gone before it, and that surrounds it in its present. A key question for people as they judge something is the extent to which it is original or not: this of course can be subject to much disagreement. As with Guilford, Vernon's view reflects a belief that creativity resides with the 'person'. However, the idea that creativity has to be 'accepted' by others points to later ideas about the significance of the societal context for creativity.

One of the most influential figures in the creativity research world is Mihály Csikszentmihályi. Csikszentmihályi's early work (1990) focused on personality, motivation and the discovery of new problems. His research with several hundred artists sought to understand why some produced work that would be judged to be creative, while others did not. As far as personality was concerned, it was found that more creative students had the following features: they were sensitive; they were open to experiences and impulses; they were self-sufficient and not particularly interested in social norms or acceptance. But the trait that most consistently distinguished these artists from others was 'a cold and aloof disposition' (ibid., p. 192). Even at this stage, Csikszentmihályi recognised that the fact that these were artists, and not scientists or another group of people, was significant and that these findings probably would not generalise to other groups.

Like other researchers, Csikszentmihályi and his team failed to find any relationship between traditional measures of intelligence and criteria for creative accomplishment. Csikszentmihályi realised that for many creative individuals, the *formulation* of a problem is more important than its solution. Thus, he set out to investigate the 'discovery orientation' of artists. When presented with visually interesting objects and drawing materials, a group of students were encouraged to do what they wanted, and finish when they had produced a drawing that they liked. The variables used to measure the students' discovery orientation included the number of objects that they touched: the higher the number, the more likely it was that the problem was being approached from a discovery orientation. Another variable was the number of changes the person introduced into the drawing process. Established artists and teachers rated drawings produced by students who had used discovery orientation much more highly in terms of originality than other students who had used a more predictable problem-solving approach. In terms of artistic career success, some seven years later the correlation was still significant.

Csikszentmihályi's early work through a person-centred approach led ultimately to the view that this was not the full picture. Instead, he proposed that the usual question 'what is creativity?' may have to be replaced by 'where is creativity?' (1990, p. 200). His well-known 'systems perspective' (p. 205) sees creativity as the result of interaction between three subsystems: the person, the field and the domain. The domain is a system that has a set of rules. This might be a subject, such as mathematics, or a religion, a game or a sport. For example, western classical music is a 'domain' that requires the composition of sound and silence to create pieces of music for the benefit of performers and audiences. The 'field' is part of the social system which has the power to influence the structure of the domain. Music competitions such as the Lionel Tertis International Viola Competition and Workshop are part of the way in which the field of classical music has influence. Entry to music colleges and the scholarships that they provide are also part of the influence of the field. The most important function of the field is to maintain the domain as it is, but the field will also act as a gatekeeper to allow changes to the domain to take place. The role of the person is to provide variations in the domain which will be judged by the field. Variations of this kind represent creativity.

Teresa Amabile has also made a very significant contribution to the creativity research field. Because of her dissatisfaction with standardised creativity tests, she used tests or activities in which participants did things such as make paper collages or write haiku. These were then judged for creativity and other dimensions by experts, such as studio artists and practising poets. Amabile calls this 'consensual assessment' (1990, p. 65): 'A product or response is creative to the extent that appropriate observers independently agree it is creative. Appropriate observers are those familiar with the domain in which the product was created or the response articulated' (ibid., p. 65). The conceptual definition of creativity that she used was as follows: 'A product or response will be judged as creative to the extent that (a) it is both a novel and appropriate, useful, correct, or valuable response to the task at hand, and (b) the task is heuristic rather than algorithmic' (p. 66). Amabile makes the point that although creativity is often very difficult for judges to define, they can recognise it when they see it. They also have considerable agreement about their judgements, particularly as regards products, though less so for creativity in persons or processes. She also correctly argued, in our view, that creativity is a continuous rather than a discontinuous quality which begins with everyday creativity at one end and ends with Einstein, Mozart and Picasso at the other end. The differences are not the presence of creativity per se but the abilities, cognitive styles, motivational levels and circumstances of the different people concerned.

The move away from defining creativity as a fixed entity to one that is dependent on people's judgements has relevance to the context of school classrooms. If it is possible to teach creativity, then teachers are going to play an important role. Teachers are experts in their subjects, which they have studied at degree level and beyond, and they also have significant knowledge about child development, which gives them appropriate knowledge with which to judge children's creativity, something that is akin to Craft's (2000) 'little c' creativity.

The definition of creativity that we adopt for this book is a slightly modified version of Vernon's (1989):

> **Creativity** – a person's capacity to produce new or original ideas, insights, restructurings, inventions, or artistic objects, which are accepted by suitably qualified people as being of scientific, aesthetic, social, or technological value.

If a child is to be judged as creative, then they have to demonstrate the ability to create. This means that they will demonstrate original thinking, which will often, but not always, result in tangible products. A consensual judgement has to be made as to whether creativity has taken place. In the case of schools, this judgement will normally be made by class teachers.

There are a number of other terms that are common in education and are closely related to creativity:

> **Creative teaching** – this is teaching that demonstrates original thinking and actions. Creative teaching may enhance children's creativity but may not. Teaching that is receptive to *pupils'* creativity is probably more likely to enhance children's creativity than creative teaching per se.
>
> **Teaching for creativity** – this is the kind of teaching that features in courses such as creative writing. Students are helped by teachers to be more creative in arts subjects such as music composition, art, design, etc. There is perhaps evidence here that creativity *can* be taught, or at the very least facilitated.
>
> **Creative learning** is a term that has become important in England over the last few years, and one that we address in the rest of this chapter.

Creative learning

In 1999, a report commissioned by government, called *All our futures: Creativity, culture and education* (NACCCE Report) (NACCCE, 1999), argued that a national strategy for creative and cultural education was essential to unlock the potential of every young person (we shall address the extent to which the national strategies have achieved this in Chapter 8, 'Creativity in the primary curriculum'). One of the most positive developments following the NACCCE report was the national Creative Partnerships initiative. In our view, much of the practice that emerged from the Creative Partnerships initiative was excellent; indeed, some of the examples in the remaining chapters in the book have been inspired by Creative Partnerships activities and ideas. This chapter, though, continues with its aim to explore definitions and understandings.

In the early days of Creative Partnerships, creative learning was the term that dominated its work. Its use can still be seen in the research section of the Creative Partnerships website:

> Creative Partnerships comprises a complex programme of creative learning opportunities intended to develop and mainstream creative teaching and learning, and result in changes across the school, the curriculum and the wider community.
>
> Creative Partnerships programmes are designed to challenge and develop learning practice by:
> * exploring creative risk-taking and innovation
> * exploring what education for the 21st century might be
> * evidencing and disseminating methodologies for creative learning
> * developing the capacity of the cultural and creative sectors to work effectively in schools.
>
> (Creative Partnerships, 2008, online)

The term 'creative learning' no longer appears on the 'What is Creative Partnerships?' part of the site, where the term 'creativity' is now preferred.

Creative Partnerships is the Government's flagship creativity programme for schools and young people, managed by Arts Council England and funded by the DCSF [Department for Children, Schools and Families] and DCMS [Department for Culture, Media and Sport]. It aims to develop:

- the creativity of young people, raising their aspirations and achievements
- the skills of teachers and their ability to work with creative practitioners
- schools' approaches to culture, creativity and partnership working; and
- the skills, capacity and sustainability of the creative industries.

In the early years of Creative Partnerships, Dominic Wyse and David Spendlove were involved in research which we shall describe shortly. One of the early tasks was to examine the definitions that were being used, and in particular 'creative learning', which was a term that did not appear to come from the research field of creativity that we have reviewed in this chapter. If we were to carry out research with a focus on creative learning, we wanted to know where the term originated and what it meant. What is more, if Creative Partnerships were to evaluate their work, then a clear definition seemed necessary. Spendlove and Wyse researched what teachers' and creatives' perceptions of creative learning were.

The research questions were as follows:

1. How is creative learning defined by policy makers and in the research literature?
2. What are the views of participants in two creative partnerships of the nature of creative learning?
3. What barriers are there to creativity and creative learning?
4. How successful is the research framework in supporting development of research understanding?
5. To what extent are Creative Partnerships informed by research evidence?
6. What recommendations can be made for future policy and planning?

This chapter focuses on questions 1, 2, 3 and 5.

Creative partnership I

A total of 25 primary and secondary schools were involved in creative partnership 1. All schools worked in partnership with creatives on projects that were designed to enhance pupils' creative learning. Research support for the schools was initially provided by a team of seven research mentors who had a range of subject and phase specialisms and who all worked in an education department of a university in the region. The research mentors were each allocated four days, for each of the three schools that they worked with, to support the enhancement of the evidence base for the schools' creative work. Where possible, schools were partnered with research mentors who had subject expertise related to the curriculum areas that were linked with the projects the schools were carrying out.

An introductory conference was organised to begin the process of research training for the teachers involved. The conference covered some aspects of research on creativity and some introductory methodological issues. A research framework was introduced and the team of research mentors began some preliminary planning with their schools.

The research framework identified three phases where summative documentary evidence was required. The first phase involved meetings between the mentors and the schools, and required them to agree a research plan. All schools prepared research plans based on their creative projects. The second-phase meetings involved discussions about progress, and a focus on data that had been collected and how those data might be analysed. The final-phase meetings involved preparations for a poster presentation at an annual conference, which required the schools to identify key findings from the research and more general findings about the practical aspects of the projects. The potential significance of the role of school managers in relation to creative learning resulted in the decision to hold additional interviews with eight school managers from the partnership. These interviews, which were taped and transcribed, included questions about how the headteachers defined creative learning.

Creative partnership 2

A total of 25 primary and secondary schools were involved in creative partnership 2. The authors were commissioned to carry out a substantial evaluation of the work of creative partnership 2. The evaluation methods included focus-group interviews with teachers and creatives from all the teams in the partnership, a focus-group interview with the facilitators, and analysis of documents. The documents included a self-evaluation questionnaire that all partners had to complete which encouraged reflection on the success of their creative projects. All interviews were taped and transcribed.

An introductory conference was organised to extend research training for the teachers (called 'action researchers' in creative partnership 2) and research mentors who were involved. The conference covered some aspects of research on creativity and creative learning, and some introductory methodological issues. A pro forma was devised to monitor changing perceptions of creative learning, by action researchers and creatives, to be completed at each of four phases. The research framework was introduced and the team of research mentors, consisting of three university staff and three creative professionals, began some preliminary planning with their schools.

The research framework identified four phases where summative documentary evidence was required. The first phase involved meetings between the mentors and the schools and required them to agree a research plan. All 25 schools prepared research plans based on their creative projects. The second-phase meetings discussed progress and a focus on data that had been collected. The third phase focused on analysis of data, and the final-phase meetings involved preparations for a dissemination event.

Defining creative learning

The teachers', headteachers' and creatives' definitions of creative learning covered a very wide range of concepts. One of the teacher action researchers suggested that creative learning was 'fun, enjoyable, liberating, relevant, child centred, empowering, encourages development of questioning/problem-solving skills, imaginative ideas valued, learning styles provided for, inclusive, raises self-esteem/motivation/achievement, challenges ideas/beliefs'. This is arguably a powerful list of desirable aspects of teaching and learning, but to what extent is it unique to creative learning as opposed to other types of learning? Some of the participants struggled to offer a definition at all and seemed almost overawed by the potential range of the concept. Others argued from the point of view of policy and practice that the definition suggested by creative partnerships had changed since the inception of the initiative and that they felt that their own definition had also changed on the basis of things that they read and the influence of initiatives that were contemporaneous with Creative Partnerships. Evidence of difficulties in defining creative learning were revealed in discussions, where participants sometimes fell back on concrete descriptions of their creative project work, perhaps lacking the confidence and understanding to engage with the abstraction of the definition. So, one of the most common responses when trying to articulate a definition of creative learning was one of uncertainty.

The other equally common response was to suggest that creative learning was mainly about new approaches to teaching. One headteacher went so far as to say that the phrase 'learning styles' should be used in place of creative or creativity. The different approaches to teaching that were suggested included cross-curricular teaching; focusing on the child, not the content of the curriculum; and hands-on learning – all informed by different planning styles which were influenced by partners from the creative sector. If creative learning means different teaching and/or learning styles, it is difficult to determine how the impact of creative partnerships might be different from countless other initiatives that have attempted to change teacher practice. Our perception was that the word 'creative' should be distinct, reflecting something genuinely different rather than only a more routine change in teacher practice.

We saw particular significance in the link between previous research suggesting that creativity is enhanced when pupils are given more control and ownership of the curriculum and some of the participants' definitions of creative learning. One of the teacher action researchers emphasised children's curiosity leading to ownership: 'The moment when children want to find out more because they're curious about whatever it is you're discussing. . . . So they're not thinking I've got to do this for all the reasons that normally they think they have to.' Other participants emphasised that learning should be student led and open-ended, where the pupils took ownership in order to make the learning more personally relevant. The idea of learning without restriction was also quite a strong theme in the answers. Some participants highlighted the use of the imagination, which we saw as a neglected concept that might more appropriately describe some examples of learning than the term 'creativity'. The idea that risk taking was important was also referred to quite frequently.

Barriers to creative learning

Craft (2005) suggested that barriers to the development of creativity in education relate to the 'technisisation' of teaching, the limitations of emerging technologies, conflicts in policy and practice, and limitations stemming from centrally defined pedagogical practice. In our research, the responses fell into three categories of barriers: statutory, organisational and pedagogical.

Barriers attributed to statutory requirements included statutory tests with an emphasis upon 'attainment rather than achievement', the National Curriculum, the literacy and numeracy strategies, and the existence of an 'audit culture'. A particular constraint that was frequently highlighted was the demands of OfSTED (Office for

Standards in Education) school inspections, which have had a strong influence on school policy. There was a feeling that creativity was not sufficiently emphasised as part of the OfSTED inspection framework; as one headteacher noted, 'they've got their eyes fixed on the plastic plates that are spinning and they take their eyes off . . . the bone china ones'.

Organisational barriers were associated with competing demands that existed in schools. This meant that it was often difficult to arrange cross-faculty/department work in schools, especially if there was limited or poor support from headteachers and/or senior management teams. Another barrier, highlighted particularly by some head-teachers, was that of parental influence. It was felt that parents often had a clear view of what they expected from education but that these views sometimes conflicted with the views of schools – exemplified by the suggestion that some parents felt that 'what you should be doing in schools is not prancing around the hall pretending that you're a Roman soldier'.

Pedagogical barriers included the concept of playing safe. Although teachers wanted to take risks, the effects of accountability were felt in many ways: accountability to children, to parents and to headteachers. The difficulties of moving away from playing safe was reflected in the views of a school senior manager who felt teachers had become deskilled: 'I think some people are so entrenched in a way of delivering the curriculum that they would feel very vulnerable [if] given too much freedom'; this perhaps meant that teachers were unable to model the very creative attributes they were meant to be encouraging.

A further pedagogical barrier was revealed in the context of support from creatives (e.g. dancers, artists, etc.). It was felt that although their contributions were valued, the creatives sometimes lacked understanding of children's development, appropriate pedagogy, and issues such as school health and safety practice. When one listened to both creatives' and teachers' observations about this issue, it was apparent that both sides were capable of exaggerating these tensions and that their resolution was a natural feature of the stronger partnerships, and this process of resolution was beneficial to all parties.

Discussion

One of the limitations of the data about participants' perceptions of barriers to creative learning was that the data were collected in the context of a lack of agreement about what creative learning was. Consequently, we tempered our conclusions with the view that perceived barriers were influenced by a partial understanding. However, amid much uncertainty there seemed to be an overriding feeling that creative learning represented something less formal and less restrictive than previous practice. Given that this was the case, the two most significant barriers that were identified were the assessment system and the formal curriculum. The dangers of a narrow curriculum resulting from high-stakes testing mechanisms are well rehearsed both in recent times and even at the time of the English revised code of regulations (see Chapter 8). The national literacy and numeracy strategies, as part of the formal curriculum, were seen as a particularly strong barrier to creative learning.

The most significant finding from the research was that the term 'creative learning' lacked a stable definition and consequently meant many different things to practitioners, policy makers and researchers. The most common response from the participants in our research was the suggestion that creative learning was simply a new learning style.

As a result of this finding, we attempted to offer a working definition of creative learning by combining the views of participants with our synthesis of previous research. We arrived at the following definition of creative learning:

> Creative learning is learning that leads to new or original thinking that is accepted by appropriate observers as being of value.

This was originally offered as a working definition because it seemed to us, on the basis of our work with Creative Partnerships, that it was something that was needed if creative practice and research on creative learning were to be rigorous. The definition stresses thinking, rather than products – a reflection of the belief that all creative learning requires a distinct process of thought. There may be a tangible product as an outcome but there may not be; however, observation of the development of tangible products can be an aid to evaluating whether creative thinking is taking place.

The definition that we put forward seems to have been helpful, as can be seen in David Feldman's introductory comments and by Craft, Cremin and Burnard's chapter in their excellent book *Creative learning 3–11* (2008), an account of continuing research on creative learning. The scope of the book is particularly broad in order to fulfil its purpose of 'documenting creative learning'. A breadth of possibilities is something that also characterises the work of Banaji and Burn (2006), whose report for Creative Partnerships suggests different 'rhetorics of creativity'. This work productively reminds us that different contexts and traditions produce different ideas about creativity. However, we are not convinced by their argument that creativity will be seen more productively through such rhetorics than through characterisations that seek to endorse particular definitions. It seems to us that agreement on how creativity is defined is the starting point for understanding how it appears in a range of contexts, and particularly in classrooms.

Feldman (2008) makes the important point that specifying, even in a preliminary way, what the terms 'creative' and 'learning' mean and how they relate to each other may help us to better understand creative learning. We agree with this proposition, hence our attempt to clarify creativity and show possible links with learning throughout this book. Feldman and Benjamin (2006) point significantly to the positive influence that early childhood educators have had on maintaining creativity in their work with children. At the same time, they caution that uncritical thinking about particular trends in practice, which could include creative learning, will not serve us well. Duffy's (2006) excellent book is an example of the continuing importance of creativity in the early years. For children in the primary phase, creativity has struggled more to have an established place. We hope our book might make a small contribution to this struggle.

2 Organising teaching for creativity

In Chapter 8, we shall examine how control of the curriculum has been increasingly strengthened by government. Although this is not the ideal context for creativity to develop, there are still considerable freedoms, even within the statutory requirements of the National Curriculum, to personalise what and how we teach in the primary school. It appears that a battle is going on between different stakeholders in government. So, at times there is encouragement and praise for creativity, whereas at other times it seems to be submerged under other high-stakes requirements. The good news is that confident and effective teachers can still find many opportunities for creativity in their classrooms. Although many of the issues covered in this chapter are not unique to creativity, we consider them to be part of the classroom and school environment (and thinking) necessary to foster creativity through your curriculum.

Statutory frameworks

Let us look at the National Curriculum itself. While it delineates what must be taught in each subject, surprisingly little in the Programmes of Study is content based – the main exceptions being science, history and geography. Although there are expectations in relation to English and mathematics via the Primary National Strategy Frameworks, the National Curriculum does not give specific requirements for the number of hours that must be given to any subject, nor what proportion of the academic year must be given over to them. Importantly from a creativity perspective, it does not tell practitioners *how* they should teach, nor does it prevent cross-curricular learning. The Qualifications and Curriculum Authority (QCA), in the early days of the National Curriculum, produced suggested schemes of work for delivering the statutory requirements, and some teachers, wrongly, have taken these as being the *only* ways of interpreting the Programmes of Study.

Why not start from a different National Curriculum perspective? Key Skills and Thinking Skills also have to be covered; these can open up the door for personalising the curriculum.

You perhaps will not be surprised to hear that we are most interested in the 'creative thinking skills' column of Table 2.1. Here is official encouragement for children to generate ideas and use their imagination. However, the idea of 'identifying problems' is also significant for creativity, as we showed in Chapter 1.

Table 2.1 *National Curriculum thinking skills and key skills*

NATIONAL CURRICULUM THINKING SKILLS

Information processing skills	Reasoning skills	Enquiry skills	Creative thinking skills	Evaluation skills
Locating and collecting relevant information	Giving reasons for opinions and actions	Asking relevant questions	Generating and extending ideas	Evaluating judgement
Sorting and classifying	Drawing inferences and making deductions	Posing and defining problems	Suggesting hypotheses	Judging the value of what they read, hear and do
Sequencing	Using precise language to explain what they think	Planning what to do and how to research	Applying imagination	Developing criteria for judging the value of their own and others' work or ideas
Comparing and contrasting	Making judgements and decisions informed by reasons or evidence	Predicting outcomes and anticipating consequences	Looking for alternative outcomes	Having confidence in their judgements
Analysing part–whole relationships		Testing conclusions and improving ideas		

NATIONAL CURRICULUM KEY SKILLS

Application of number	Communication	Improving own learning and performance	Information technology	Problem solving	Working with others
Interpreting numerical information	Discussions	Setting targets	Using ICT to find information	Confirming/ identifying problems and options	Planning work
Carrying out calculations	Presenting	Using a plan	Using ICT to develop information	Planning and trying out options	Working towards objectives
Interpreting results and presenting findings – generally	Reading and obtaining information	Reviewing progress and achievements	Using ICT to present information	Checking whether problems have been solved	Identifying objectives
Using graphs and charts	Reading and summarising information				Reviewing work
Using diagrams	Reading and synthesising information				Working in groups
Using maps	Writing documents in general				Working in pairs
Using other methods	Drafting/redrafting information				
	Organising information				

Excellence and enjoyment

The Primary National Strategy document *Excellence and enjoyment* (DfES, 2003) is a good example of the tensions that exist in the primary curriculum. On the one hand, the more rigid literacy and mathematics frameworks must be followed, but at the same time considerable freedoms to innovate are also suggested. *Excellence and enjoyment* partially recognised the need for diversity within schools and the need for teachers to express themselves in such a way as to motivate their pupils.

An important element of *Excellence and enjoyment* was the listing of the Key Aspects of Learning that we should be aiming to cover in our teaching. Table 2.2 organises the Key Aspects into a grid that you will find useful for the skills-based planning to be outlined later in this chapter. Here we see another reminder about the importance of creative thinking – so much so that we would wish to see it given greater prominence than being just one of many other key aspects of learning. One thing that our exploration of definitions of creativity showed in Chapter 1 was the complexities and hence the need for a main focus on creativity rather than as one of many options.

The Primary National Strategy Frameworks for Literacy and Mathematics, while non-statutory, are strongly recommended by government, so schools have to present coherent and evidence-based arguments if they decide against implementation. However, even if they are the predominant way the school organises English and maths, it is possible to integrate the framework objectives within the wider development of skills, knowledge and understanding through cross-curricular learning.

Ideally, the leadership and management team will involve all staff in determining the policy for teaching and learning within the school, using guidelines from *Excellence and enjoyment* to identify the particular ethos, values and vision that makes the school individual. This enables a whole-school approach to be developed over a period of time, where cross-curricular learning, alongside the specific teaching of particular skills, knowledge and understanding, can ensure opportunities for creativity development.

Timetables

Some blocks of time are predetermined by the use of shared spaces such as the hall or the computer suite, by assemblies or by the availability of support staff. Apart from this, it is possible for teachers to have a large amount of autonomy within their individual timetabling. This will allow for more creative approaches to teaching and learning. A traditional timetable stating given times for individual subjects does not reflect cross-curricular teaching. If we want children to see links between areas, we must teach them in such a way as to make that possible. In previous decades, the words 'Topic' or 'Project' would have appeared on many primary timetables (see later in this chapter), rather than there being separate blocks labelled 'Geography', 'History' or 'Science', for example. While this approach had much to commend it in terms of personalised and cross-curricular learning, it could lack structured progression. There was the chance that unintended repetition of subject matter would happen as children passed through the years of the primary school. Sometimes, in an attempt to ensure that *all* learning was based on the chosen theme, some rather tenuous links could be made which were rather artificial and not particularly beneficial for learning and teaching. However, at its best, topic work can provide a meaningful and exciting context for a range of work. Some examples will be given later, when we look at planning.

Table 2.2 *Primary National Strategy key aspects of learning*

Inquiry	Problem solving	Creative thinking	Information processing	Reasoning	Evaluation
Ask and answer relevant questions	Recognise and explain a problem and hypothesise about solutions	Use imagination to come up with original ideas and change ideas to suit the purpose	Find and organise information from a wide range of sources, including books and ICT	Use own knowledge and experience to predict and generalise, and apply this to new situations	Recognise that evaluation requires criteria against which to make judgements and decide which criteria are important and why
Form plans and decide on research strategies	Plan and try out possible solutions, using appropriate tools	Speculate about possibilities and think about their consequences	Search for information and use alternative strategies if a search fails	Make decisions on the quality, reliability and validity of evidence, data and information	Make independent, critical judgements against criteria and justify own decisions
Improve own ideas and suggest improvements to others' ideas	Change actions if necessary to improve steps being taken to solve the problem	Question what is being told and suggest own ideas	Sort by multiple criteria, classify, summarise and synthesise information	Synthesise, analyse and apply evidence, data and information in a variety of ways, including dealing with conflicting evidence	Amend judgements when appropriate in the light of further evidence
Plan, design and carry out an enquiry	Evaluate solutions by reflecting on the process taken and the outcomes	Take risks and change ideas	Record information in a variety of ways	Identify patterns, sequences and cause and effect	Evaluate progress in own learning and offer ideas for improvement
	Make judgements about the quality of the solution and the processes taken, using relevant success criteria	Judge own ideas and outcomes against the purpose	Explain how a given factor affected a situation or test	Compare and discriminate between ideas	Talk about own strengths and areas for development
			Identify the relationship between factors		

Table 2.2 continued

Self-awareness	Managing feelings	Motivation	Empathy	Social skills	Communication
Talk about own strengths and areas for development	Use appropriate words to explain own feelings	Work for the pleasure of learning, creating or doing in its own right	Anticipate when other people may feel worried or nervous	Describe what helps own group to work well together	Organise and shape a talk, making connections between ideas and drawing on different points of view
Make up own mind and make decisions based on different opinions	Explain own feelings in new situations and have strategies to cope	Persevere even when experiencing difficulties, and try additional and alternative approaches	Know how others may be feeling when they are in different situations	Listen to, respond to and interact with others	Use standard English appropriately
Motivate self to work well on own and ask for help when needed	Use strategies with uncomfortable feelings to calm self when necessary	Ignore interruptions and carry on working	Help others to feel valued and welcomed	Learn with others, taking on different responsibilities and tasks	Use persuasive techniques deliberately to influence the listener
	Use past experiences to help control own feelings in difficult situations	Set own goals and work towards them as well as working towards goals set by others	Recognise similarities and differences between self and other people	Predict when there may be conflict and take action to prevent it happening	Use talk imaginatively, engaging the attention and interest of the listener
		Break down long-term goals into short-term goals and evaluate own progress towards these	Show value and respect to other people by taking an interest in what they say and do	Discuss politely even when other people have different opinions	Make use of a variety of ways to challenge and accept criticism
		Recognise when own goals have been achieved and gain pleasure from experiencing success	Recognise and label the feelings and behaviours of others	Act appropriately according to company, time and place	Negotiate and make decisions taking account of alternatives and consequences
		Make decisions about ways to work	Describe how own mood can affect other people in the room		

If a cross-curricular approach is not possible, try organising your timetable so that lessons follow on from one another in a logical and linked way. Science could follow maths so that, for example, the mathematical skills or concepts you have just taught can be applied in an appropriate scientific context. Or you could work on letter writing in a literacy session knowing that the following history session will use those skills where the children write a letter in role as a historic character. Even better perhaps is to double-count time, using the content-based elements of the curriculum as the vehicle for key skills. In this way, for example, scientific facts could be used as part of problem solving and investigation, or geographical knowledge could form the basis for report writing – and all subjects can enhance ICT and presentation skills.

It is often a good idea to vary timetables from week to week. One week you may spend a whole day on science-based work, while the following week may see a day being spent on completing an art project; or several days' maths lessons could be combined into a day spent carrying out an in-depth maths-based investigation linked to the local environment, while the following week might give more time for working on a sustained piece of writing. This approach to timetabling can provide a stronger sense of cohesion for learning.

Ways of delivering the curriculum

Many ways of delivering the curriculum have been tried over the years, so it is worth looking at some of the better-known models to see what they may have to offer us today.

The menu system

Popular in the 1960s and 1970s, before the advent of the National Curriculum, the menu system was based on a series of activities designed to be completed within the week. The first morning of the week required the teacher to explain enough of the activities so that the children could begin working. However, other activities could be added during the week and further explanations or developments of activities in progress could be offered. Some activities were process-based ones so that, once the children were familiar with them, they could be reused by varying some of the content from week to week. The classroom was set up so that all resources were available, often in particular areas of the room. In the menu system's most liberal form, the children could then select the order in which they completed the activities and determine their own pace, keeping a record of what they had covered as the week progressed and, of course, aiming to complete the full range by the end of the week. The menu system was built on mixed-ability teaching, although some teachers structured it a little more by on occasion grouping children according to abilities, so that direct teaching of ability groups could be timetabled across the week, while the rest of the class selected activities from the menu. Teachers had to gradually introduce the routines to children, so it was common to start with a limited choice of perhaps two activities, and then, as the children began to understand the rules and routines, more choice could be introduced.

Benefits of this system were that children were afforded choice, thus taking on a degree of responsibility for their own learning which fostered independence. There was also real scope for individualised in-depth learning and teaching, including tasks that could even span more than one day if appropriate. The disadvantages were that the physical organisation of the system was not easy in some classrooms, and depended upon all resources being available all the time. It could take some time at the start of the week to explain the week's work to the children, and inevitably there were some children who did not benefit from the flexible structure and struggled to complete the week's work.

It is possible for you to incorporate elements of the menu system into your classroom, avoiding the disadvantages. For example, you could have a series of linked activities for the children to choose from. Box 2.1 is an example linking Literacy, Drama and Art.

Box 2.1   Dear Greenpeace

Text: *Dear Greenpeace* by Simon James

Learning focus: Letter writing

Teacher focus: How to construct letters. The difference between formal and informal letters.

Linked activities: a In pairs, read out aloud the letters between Emily, the girl in the story, and Greenpeace. Use an appropriate tone of voice.

b Read a selection of letters provided by the teacher, sorting them into formal and informal, listing the differences between them.

c Write a letter to either Emily or Greenpeace from the whale's point of view.

d In pairs, create a short scene where Emily is being interviewed for the local newspaper or TV news.

e Write a letter to Greenpeace from one of Emily's parents, stating their concerns.

f Write an informal letter from Emily to a friend after the story has ended.

g Create a painting or collage showing the ideal place for a whale to live.

An alternative, in any subject area, could be to offer a choice of activities that *must* be completed alongside several that *might* be done, effectively providing extension work at different levels.

The Integrated Day

The integrated day was popular pre-1988, before the National Curriculum. It was a topic-based approach to learning whereby teachers had the freedom to select their own curriculum content within relatively loose parameters for the curriculum specified by local authorities. In this model, as many subject links as possible were made, with the topic leading the learning.

The main advantage of this system was its cross-curricular nature, whereby learning was 'joined up', enabling children to see links between subjects. This allowed for in-depth study within a holistic context. Specific skills were taught as needed rather than being pre-planned. Because of the nature of the work, strict timetabling was rarely necessary, thus allowing time for activities to be completed, providing a sense of satisfaction and the opportunity for evaluation and reflection. Such a cross-curricular approach is still very valuable, although we would now have to pay close attention to the content requirements of the National Curriculum and bring skills development very much to the forefront of our planning. Figure 2.1 is an example of planning reflecting teaching the integrated day.

The work wheel

Sometimes referred to as a 'carousel', this method was also used pre-1988. A selection of four or five activities, often related to a topic, were prepared by the teacher. Mixed-ability groups were established and were directed to start the day with a particular activity. Sometimes the teacher then gave time limits so that all the groups rotated at a particular moment such as after a break. It was also possible in classrooms that had enough space for pupils who had completed one activity to rotate to the next activity before their peers.

The system worked best where additional adults were available to help supervise and guide the groups who were not working with the teacher, and where there were sufficient resources to support three or four groups working independently. It was

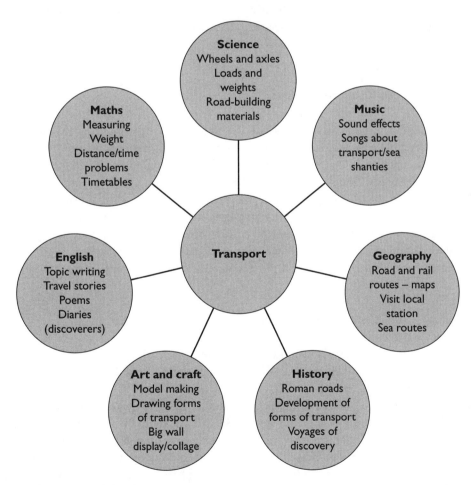

Figure 2.1 Integrated day plan – transport

necessary for children to be fairly self-supporting during independent work, so that learning strategies for working quietly and independently were vital. Some children found this quite difficult.

It was hard for teachers to plan a continuous programme of worthwhile independent activities, and many became concerned that a proportion of work carried on independently was not moving children on in their learning. Ultimately, many teachers streamlined the system to have fewer groups, or to use their own skills to be available to support more of the groups during a session. This method can work very well where, for example, three main activities are happening at the same time with the class divided into three groups. Maybe all activities will be completed in one session, or they could be spread over a day or three consecutive days. The system suffered from similar criticisms to those levelled at the integrated day and because the teacher had to monitor so many different activities at the same time. Thus, it was something of a surprise to find it recommended in the early days of the National Literacy Strategy, where it was seen as a good way to organise reading and writing groups working independently while the teacher focused on a guided group.

Although we have illustrated some of the limitations of these alternative ways of organising the curriculum, we do think they offer considerable benefits for fostering creativity. All forms of classroom organisation have limitations. For that reason, it is a good idea to use different ways of delivering the curriculum so that the limitations of one are cancelled out by another, and because the changing patterns are likely to be more interesting for the children in your class.

Developing a skills-based curriculum

The National Curriculum lists the knowledge, skills and understanding that we must ensure children have by the end of their primary schooling. Equipping children for the twenty-first century, and the potential changes they will encounter, depends upon their having a secure base of transferable skills. Moving away from planning based on *content* to planning based on *skills* is an important shift in how we perceive learning and teaching. In order to do this, basing cross-curricular planning on the requirements listed in the National Curriculum, rather than relying on, for example, QCA unit plans, will give you the freedom to inject your own, and your pupils', ideas into your teaching.

Begin by selecting a topic that provides your context for teaching. For example, you might choose contexts such as:

- History – The Tudors, Famous People, or Houses and Homes
- Science – Forces and Energy, or Habitats
- Geography – Maps and Plans or Local Settlements
- Literacy – Heroes and Heroines, Adventures or Fantasy Worlds.

Talk to the children in your class and ask them about topics they would like to study and the kinds of things that they know and would like to learn about the topic. Having chosen your theme, draw a 'spider diagram' or 'topic web', each branch listing the areas to be covered by the topic. This exercise will enable you to develop an overall view of the work you will be incorporating into your unit, lasting between a half and a whole term. Figure 2.2 shows an example of a teacher's topic web.

Figure 2.2 Example of a topic web

Music
historical to
• compose pieces
• show events

Geog
Map work
England • London/York
• Spain etc

Art
↳ Firework - silhouette
↳ Art history
  famous pics
  emotions / bias
  PSHE opinions

MAIN FOCUS
• Guy Fawkes - events
leading to Bonfire
Night.

END OF
TOPIC ASSESSMENT.

• Dress up day
• Act out events
• Discussions/philosophy
• Olden day feast
  ↳ JK cooking group.

Whizz, Pop, Bang!
Who's that Guy?

Literacy
• Firework poetry (set scene)
• Creative story telling
  (humanities based stories)

make story
bags.
link to
G.reading?

Art
Turn Classrooms
into above
Houses of Parl e
below.
Swap rooms for
Drama / story
telling etc.

Science/DT
making buggies
& make
fire engines

Electricity
Circuits
(bulb/buzzer/
switch)

ICT
Roamer
• Beebot as
  fire engines
  direct/
  program

It can be seen from Figure 2.2 that the teachers have thought in a cross-curricular fashion, looking for appropriate links between subject areas. Having one particular subject in mind to stimulate the planning does not stifle the opportunity for linking creatively to other areas of the curriculum. By making such links, the learning is both deepened and broadened for the children.

Next, identify and highlight, on photocopies of the grids provided earlier, the National Curriculum Key Skills and Thinking Skills, and the Key Aspects of Learning that you will be covering within your topic. You will see from the completed example in Table 2.3 that the next phase is to select the key subject skills taken from the National Curriculum, identifying, in this case, two main focus subjects and several supporting subject areas that will be covered by the topic. Your initial topic web planning will provide the context for this.

Table 2.3 is an example of how the topic web was used to inform medium-term planning. From this medium-term plan, the teachers were able to make their more detailed short-term plans, using a flexible timetable. In order to teach the Key Skills on the medium-term plan, they selected some activities that all children would be expected to complete, as well as several optional activities that *might* be completed – in effect providing extension activities for the higher attaining children, or indeed alternative activities for the lower attaining children.

A second example of this style of planning is shown in Figure 2.3. This was planned for a Key Stage 2 unit of work that was given the catchy title of 'Treasure Seekers'. It involved children from Years 3 and 4 working together with the local museum in Mildenhall, Suffolk. As the children were studying the Romans and the museum has a replica set of Roman artefacts found locally, known as 'the Mildenhall Treasure', teachers Helen and Rachel worked closely with museum staff to stimulate learning while covering a wide range of curriculum content but specifically focusing on developing skills.

Learning styles

In recent years, the idea of varied learning styles has become popular. This popularity has been seen in concepts such as VAK (visual, auditory and kinaesthetic) learning styles and in the idea of personalised learning.

Auditory learning is traditionally well catered for, but visual learning less so. To support visual learning, you can use stimuli in the form of puppets or artefacts, and create images and text on the interactive whiteboard. Practical activities to enable kinaesthetic learning sometimes begin to take a back seat as children progress through school; this is often when lack of the right kind of learning can lead at worst to disruptive behaviour and at best to a lack of engagement and motivation. Fortunately, creative approaches espouse learning by doing, so that investigative tasks often necessitate physical involvement. This may be as simple as moving to different parts of the room or building for different elements of the learning, such as might be found in a maths trail, for example. Physical drama, story props, maths resources, historical artefacts, games, or science resources are all channels that allow for kinaesthetic learning.

The work of Howard Gardner encouraged people to rethink the concept of intelligence. Our society has conditioned us into thinking that intelligence and academic achievement are fixed and limited concepts, but Gardner suggested that there are different types of intelligence:

Table 2.3 *Year 2 planning*

Medium-term planning
Whizz, pop, bang – who's that Guy?

Skills to be covered

Theme	Year group	Date
Guy Fawkes	**2**	**Autumn 2nd half-term**
National Curriculum thinking skills	Information Processing – Comparing and contrasting Reasoning – Give reasons for opinions and actions Reasoning – Make judgements and decisions informed by reasons or evidence Enquiry – Predict outcomes and anticipate consequences Creative thinking – Look for alternative outcomes Creative thinking – Apply imagination Evaluation – Develop criteria for judging the value of their own and others' work or ideas	
National Curriculum key skills	**Application of number – using maps. *Using diagrams*** Communication – Discussions. Presenting. Reading and summarising. Writing documents in general. Improving own learning performance – reviewing progress and achievements. Information technology – using ICT to present information. Problem solving – confirming and identifying problems and options. Planning and trying out options. Checking whether problem is solved. Working with others – working in groups/pairs. Working towards objectives.	
Key aspects of learning	See separate highlighted sheet.	

Subject skills

History	*Science*
Chronological understanding – Place events and objects in chronological order.	*Science 1*
Knowledge and understanding – Recognise why people did things, why events happened and what happened as a result.	Ideas and evidence – Make observations and measurements, while trying to answer a question.
Historical interpretation – Identify different ways in which the past is represented.	Planning – Ask and decide how they might find answers. Recognise when a test or comparison is unfair.
Historical enquiry – To ask and answer questions about the past.	*Obtaining and presenting evidence*
Organisation and communication – To select from knowledge of history and communicate it in a variety of ways.	Follow simple instructions to control the risks to themselves and others. Communicate what happened in a variety of ways.
Breadth of study – Past events from the history of Britain and the wider world.	*Considering evidence and evaluating* Compare what happened with their predictions and try to explain it, drawing on their knowledge and understanding.
	Science 4: Electricity Everyday appliances that use electricity. Simple circuits involving batteries, wires, bulbs and other components. How a switch can be used to break a circuit.

Table 2.3 *continued*

Other subject areas to be covered

Literacy	Poetry (one week linked to fireworks) (political chants) Humanities-based stories (focusing on creative storytelling)
ICT	*Finding things out* – To gather information from a variety of sources. *Developing ideas and making things happen* – How to plan and give instructions to make things happen. *Reviewing, modifying and evaluating work as it progresses* – To review what they have done to help them develop their ideas. *Breadth of study* – explore a variety of ICT tools.
Art	*Exploring and developing ideas* – To record from first hand observation, experience and imagination and explore ideas. *Investigating and making art, craft and design* – To represent observations, ideas and feelings and design and make images and artefacts. *Evaluating and developing work* – To review what they and others have done and say what they think and feel about it. *Knowledge and understanding* – Differences and similarities in the work of artists, craftspeople and designers in different times and cultures. *Breadth of study* – To work on their own and collaborate with others, on projects in two and three dimensions and on different scales.
Design and technology	*Developing, planning and communicating ideas* – Communicate their ideas using a variety of methods (drawing, making models). *Talk about their ideas.* Generate their ideas by drawing on their own and other people's experiences. *Working with tools, equipment, materials and components to make a quality product* – Select tools, techniques and materials for making their product from a range suggested by the teacher. *Evaluating process and product* – Talk about their ideas, saying what they like and dislike. *Breadth of study* – Focused practical tasks that develop a range of techniques, skills, processes and knowledge. Design and make assignments for food.
Geography	*Geographic enquiry and skills* – To use globes, maps and plans. *Knowledge and understanding of place* – To identify and describe where places are.
Music	*Controlling sounds through singing and playing and performing skills* – To use their voices expressively by singing songs and speaking chants and rhymes. *Breadth of study* – a range of live and recorded music from different times and cultures.

Areas to be taught outside

Physical education	Please see separate planning.
Religious education	Please see separate planning.
Personal, social and health education	Some links with 'Getting on and falling out' topic.

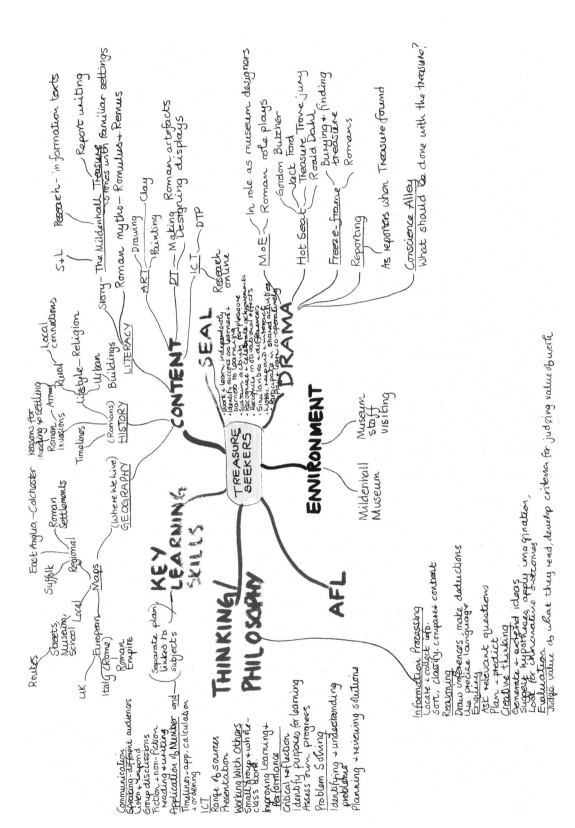

Figure 2.3 'Treasure seekers' – an example of cross-curricular planning

- linguistic intelligence
- musical intelligence
- logical-mathematical intelligence
- spatial intelligence
- bodily-kinaesthetic intelligence
- the personal intelligences.

The last-named of these refers to intelligences that are 'directed towards other persons' and 'directed towards oneself'. If the concept of multiple intelligences seems strange, think of a world-class sportsperson and consider what their particular skills enable them to do better than others. We might say that such a person possesses an enhanced bodily-kinaesthetic intelligence.

Gardner's multiple intelligence theory is built on the logical idea that it is not sensible to express intelligence as a single entity or number such as an intelligence quotient (IQ). People reveal different kinds of intelligences depending on their abilities and the tasks they frequently engage in. However, the attempt to simplify Gardner's extensive exploration in his book has resulted in some highly questionable practices. The worst of these has resulted in the *labelling* of children as one of Gardner's seven intelligences. You can almost imagine badges saying, 'I am spatial'! The best use of the theory of multiple intelligences is when it enables teachers to see the most positive features of their children's abilities. It can also help children to reflect more on their own strengths and areas for development. It provides a tool for valuing every child's intellectual contribution. It also encourages teachers to be more varied in the way they teach, which is likely to result in children being more interested in their learning.

Box 2.2 offers a more child-friendly way of describing Gardner's intelligences, a way that was developed as part of classroom work with children. Table 2.4 gives an example of how these intelligences were applied to a geography lesson by a teacher.

Box 2.2   Smarts

Think about the kind of 'smart' you are. Give yourself a score between 1 and 5 for each one: 1 = I'm not strong on this; 5 = I'm strong on this.

Word smart

You are interested in language, including reading and writing. You like learning other languages. You enjoy word puzzles and/or playing games like Scrabble, or doing crosswords. You prefer learning through text and print.

Music smart

You are interested in listening to music and talking about music. You enjoy playing musical instruments and/or singing. You like inventing new music. You prefer learning that is supported by sound and music.

Logic smart

You are interested in numbers, finding patterns, and solving problems and puzzles. You find charts and graphs interesting. You work in a logical way, and enjoy finding the 'right' answer. You prefer learning in a logical, carefully planned way.

Space smart

You are interested in drawing, painting, model making and/or working with textiles. You can spot things in pictures that other people might miss. You prefer to learn when you see images or can draw pictures or use symbols and diagrams.

Body smart

You like sport or dance. You find it hard to sit still and like to fiddle with objects, or doodle when you are listening or working. You enjoy making things and like using construction apparatus. You prefer learning by making and doing.

Person smart

You like to spend time with groups of people. You can often tell when your friends are feeling sad, angry, worried or excited. You prefer learning when you are part of a group.

Self smart

You don't mind being on your own. You can set yourself goals and work hard to achieve them. You prefer learning on your own.

Table 2.4 *Using maps and plans: work based on maps, plans and directions*

Type of intelligence	Possible activity
Word smart	Write a set of directions between two places of your own choice, providing explanations of landmarks along the way
Music smart	Choose a route between two places on a map. Compose a piece of music using tuned and untuned percussion, to represent the route.
Logic smart	Use an OS map to measure the distances between your home and ten places you might visit. Put them into a list from shortest to longest journey. How long would it take you to (a) walk and (b) drive between these places?
Space smart	Use a section of a map as the basis for a collage.
Body smart	Plan a fitness trail around the school grounds to include exercises for different parts of the body. Make a map of your route.
Person smart	Make a list of Things to Do and Things to Avoid for someone you know, walking between two places of your choice. You could include lists of what to wear or carry depending upon different types of weather.
Self smart	Choose a location on the OS map of an area you do not know. Using the information on the map, write about what it might be like to live in that location. How would it feel at different times of the day, night or year? Would you want to change anything about it?

3 Everyday creativity

In the previous chapter, we thought about ways in which the whole curriculum could be delivered. In this chapter, we zoom in on the classroom. For some teachers, the idea of creativity can seem somewhat daunting. The thrust of this chapter shows you that creativity can begin in small ways, with the kinds of things that can be a part of every day.

If children are to develop their creativity, you need to set up your classroom so that it welcomes innovation and experimentation, is open to the consideration of unusual ideas and encourages children to have a go without the fear of being undervalued. Your pupils will not flourish creatively if they are regarded as passive learners; we have come a long way from the notion that children are empty vessels to be filled only with the knowledge from the teacher. Set the scene by helping children to paddle in the shallows before swimming in the deeper water. In this chapter, we provide a variety of starting points and ideas to help creativity happen every day.

Organisation and the ethos of the classroom

Arranging your space

Begin by taking an objective view of your usual teaching space. Simply rearranging the furniture can have an impact on your teaching and the pupils' learning. Consider different ways of fitting tables together instead of the usual square or rectangle. How about arranging the space to create different working zones? You could have science, writing and maths zones, with each one having all the necessary resources as appropriate for the area. How about a quiet study zone, or an art zone? In the past, primary classrooms used to be organised like this; in the early years this still happens. Go and spend some time in a nursery!

Look at the ways in which space in the outside world is utilised, for example the upright divisions between tables to create more private areas in restaurants or libraries. Try using this idea to separate adjacent tables with temporary cardboard dividers or garden mesh or trellis, about one and a half metres high, so creating a personal wall space for the children on either side. Not only will this provide a simple study area to help with increased concentration, but it can be personalised by the children with timetables, reminders, notes, etc.

Resources

If you are to develop more open-ended processes in your classroom, where the children often direct the learning, you cannot always predict particular resources that may be needed. In order to facilitate creative use of resources, you should have an organised space where tools and resources are easily found by anyone who needs them. There are obvious items to include such as a range of types and sizes of paper, and mark-making equipment including pencils, pens, felt-tips, highlighters, and wax and pencil crayons, but you should also have available basic stationery such as treasury tags, paper clips, Post-it notes, glue sticks, sticky tape and split pins, as well as equipment including staplers, pencil sharpeners, scissors, rulers and hole-punchers. Letter stencils, tracing paper, sticky labels and guideline sheets are also useful, as well as a supply of scrap paper for quick notes or trial efforts. Art supplies should include different types of brushes, sponges and objects that could be used for printing, together with ready-mix and solid poster paints and pots for water. It is a good idea to develop basic rules for using resources so that all the children have as many chances as possible to develop their creative ideas. Expensive resources need to be used appropriately. If possible, provide access to digital cameras, simple digital video recorders and small audio recording devices. Remember that the aim is to provide easy access to resources, so they need to be meticulously stored and labelled so that children can also put them away easily. However, you don't have to have everything available all the time. Some rotation of resources can help to revitalise the classroom from time to time, and also allows you to control expensive and/or fragile resources.

For research and information gathering, easy access to both books and the internet are vital. You are unlikely to have all the non-fiction you need in your classroom, so training the children in the effective use of the library is important. Don't forget, however, that for some topics, much more current information can be cheaply accessed through newspapers, magazines and free leaflets, which are easily resourced.

Creating a positive atmosphere

One of the goals of a classroom that encourages creativity is for the children to take on greater responsibility for their own learning. Daily routines can engender an ethos where independence is encouraged. This can begin as soon as children enter the room each morning, for example by initiating a system of self-registration appropriate to the age group. For the youngest children, illustrated name cards can be arranged on a table so the children can collect their name card and place it in one of two or three suitably labelled boxes – to show either that they are staying to school lunch, that they have brought a packed lunch, or that they are going home for lunch. Older children can put an appropriate symbol or letter next to their name on a class list with columns for each day of the week. The information generated can then be used by either yourself or a teaching assistant to complete the official daily registers.

Some children can find it difficult to realise or acknowledge their own learning, being more able to say what they cannot do rather than what they can do. Children who are unaware of their strengths, or of when, what and how they are learning, are less likely to work creatively. An important element of assessment for learning and in raising children's self-esteem is to help them become better at understanding their achievements, in the very broadest sense. One way to achieve this is to have a class Success Box (see Box 3.1). This idea came spontaneously from Callum, a Year 3 boy low in self-esteem and for whom a feeling of success was rare. Fortunately, his teacher not only listened to his suggestion, but used it to great effect with her class.

Box 3.1   The Success Box

Tell the children that you want to help them to celebrate their successes. To do this, you first have to agree what you mean by success. Criteria could include:

- something you feel proud of;
- something you do for the first time;
- something you feel you have improved at;
- something that was a challenge.

You should also include things that occur out of school. When any individual feels they have achieved a success, they complete a special sheet outlining the success, and put it in the box, which should be prominently displayed. The box should be opened weekly and all the successes read out. The sheets are then displayed on a Success Board for the following week, after which the children can take them home, leaving space for the next round of successes.

As part of children's developing independence, an approach to differentiation that gives them more control can be achieved by offering responsibility for choosing their own level of challenge. This works well in mathematics, where, for example, following the taught section, the usual three levels of differentiated activity are provided for the main part of the lesson, but the children are invited to select their own level, which can be explained by saying, 'If you think you need just a little more practice, choose this sheet or activity; if you are ready for a real challenge, choose this one. If you think you'd like a bit more help before you do any more, come and work here with me.' Alternatively, all activities can be put on to one sheet, with the children choosing their own starting point, or moving on whenever they feel confident that they understand.

Collaborative working

Creativity requires both periods of concentration for individuals and the opportunity to collaborate. The novelist Stephen King explained how the early stages of his writing are private but there comes a point when he is ready to show a draft to someone. For him, that first person is always his wife. Later, his editor and other publishing company professionals will collaborate in the process. While highly creative people often work individually, it is also useful to develop co-operative and collaborative working, as many of us work well when sharing ideas and expertise. Box 3.2 shows a practical way to encourage collaboration.

Box 3.2   Incentives for collaboration

One way to help children learn to work together is to have an incentive system that rewards co-operation and collaboration. As most classrooms are arranged, at least for part of the day, with children sitting in groups around tables, a table points system is simple and effective. The children choose a name for their table, perhaps linked to a particular theme, and a special laminated label is made with the name and an illustration, to be displayed on the table. Some examples might be:

- sea theme: sharks, jellyfish, orcas, stingrays, dolphins
- tree theme: oaks, sycamores, maples, chestnuts, willows
- animal theme: tigers, lions, pandas, giraffes, zebras.

A grid on the wall lists all the table groups, where a tally is kept of any table points accrued. Points can be gained for any effective collaboration such as paired or group discussions, production of group pieces in any subject, quiet work, tidy tables, or anything else you decide. At the end of each week, the winning table is identified and they keep a trophy or special object displayed on their table the following week for all to see.

The arts

Starting with books – Katie Morag and the wedding

Sometimes, launching creativity with a bang can be the best way. Try a whole day devoted to creativity inspired by a book. Mairi Hedderwick's favourite young character Katie Morag is ideal for cross-curricular working with Key Stage 1 and lower Key Stage 2 pupils. *Katie Morag and the wedding* tells the story of one of Katie Morag's grandmothers getting married on the small Scottish island where the young girl lives.

After reading and discussing the story, organise your classroom so that one area can be used as the post office on the fictional Scottish island of Struay. It should have a till, a phone, a noticeboard, weighing scales and parcels, a home-made post box with a sack and hat for the postal worker, sheets of 'stamps' (perhaps designed and printed using computers) and a section for the village shop. You could use this in itself as your starting point, with the children producing the resources needed for the shop and post office, which will cover design and technology skills, including use of ICT for making labels and posters to go on the noticeboard advertising fictional village events, or items for sale. Don't be fooled into thinking this kind of role-play activity is only for the early years! It has been used successfully right up to Year 4.

Once the context is established, a variety of activities can follow. The story revolves around Katie Morag's granny getting married, and the activities are linked to the text.

Around the rest of the room, set up tables with activities from which the children can choose. These can include the following:

- Inventing a board game based on the story. A simple track game could be made using a map of the island as a basis, with the homes of characters in the story to whom mail has to be delivered. There would, of course, be some hazards along the way. A group of children could produce the game, with guidance as necessary before it is played by both themselves and others.

- Creating maps of the island based on the children's interpretation of the story or from the book's endpapers. The maps can be as elaborate as you wish, either drawn, painted or even collage if sufficient time is allowed.
- Composing some music for the wedding celebrations. Think about the key moments for music: the fanfare for the bride; quiet music for the signing of the registers; dance music for the evening. Listen to Scottish music for techniques to be imitated, such as the Scotch snap!
- Writing postcards. Children are asked to imagine they are a guest at the wedding. They use one of the postcards of views of 'Struay' to send to a friend. These are downloaded images made to look like postcards, which can then be posted at the post office.
- Creating a menu for the café on the island. Provide downloaded images of appropriate food items for a cut-and-paste activity. Children should decide on realistic prices for the items they include on their menu. What shape should the menu be? How will they organise the presentation of the menu for the best effect?
- Designing wedding invitations.
- Writing letters between the two grannies. Katie Morag has two grannies. What would they write to each other in the run-up to the wedding? Send the finished products via the class post office.
- Making a menu for the wedding party. A selection of choices could be provided for the starters, main course and desserts from which to choose, or recipe books provided for children to create their own wedding breakfast.
- Writing something to go on the village noticeboard. This could be a For Sale item, a lost pet, or advertising a forthcoming island event.
- Making small cakes and decorating them like a wedding cake.
- Making wedding decorations. You could provide instructions for simple decorations such as cut-out and decorated hearts, good-luck horseshoes or tissue paper flowers, but children will come up with their own ideas.
- Making a plan for the wedding, outlining the events of the day so everyone knows where to be, when, and for what!
- Designing a leaflet for a helicopter flight over the island. The newly married couple enjoy just such a flight. Downloaded images of helicopters and aerial island views can be used to make leaflets advertising the flights.

Using drama – Voices in the park

Using drama as a teaching and learning technique enables children to experience events and feelings from someone else's point of view, something that they can find particularly difficult in the abstract. Drama encourages children to see possibilities beyond the immediately obvious and to build upon them (see Chapter 6, 'The Mantle of the Expert', for a more in-depth look at drama). If you are unfamiliar with using drama in your teaching, almost any of Anthony Browne's excellent and thought-provoking picture books can be used across the Key Stages. For example, *Voices in the park* was used most effectively by Bev, a literacy consultant in Suffolk, as a support for several basic drama techniques that, once you and your class have tried them, can be added to your teaching repertoire. The book is particularly strong on character and lends itself well to drama. The four 'voices' in the story are those of an upper-class mother and her son, Charles, visiting the local park, where they meet Smudge and her dad, who is unemployed.

The one thing above all others that Anthony Browne's books do is to question the usual, and make us look at things in a different way – both important elements of creativity. Start by asking pupils to look at the pictures and the text design, with no specific instruction other than to see what they can find. This exercise is designed to focus on the benefits of looking closely, and forms a basis for further work. Some of the things the children might notice are:

- unexpected images – places where Browne has added odd items, changed the usual into the unusual subtly, or explicitly;
- the use of chimpanzees where we would expect there to be humans;
- the part the endpapers play in the books, as well as the vignettes on the title pages;
- the ways in which the illustrations are framed;
- the use of close-ups;
- the selection of different fonts for the voices of the different characters;
- the positioning of the characters, and their facial expressions.

Now you are ready to read the story. Experiment with your own dramatic creativity by adopting different voices for the four characters.

1. Follow this up by asking pairs of children to choose one illustration to enact as a freeze-frame – where they replicate the pose of their chosen characters, as if frozen. Ask them to decide what their character might be thinking at that point, then walk between the pairs, and as you touch someone's shoulder, they speak the thoughts of their character. This technique is known as *thought-tracking*.
2. Next, two pairs work together, the foursome in role, as though sitting side by side on a park bench, choosing a pose they feel is appropriate to their character. Again, their thoughts can be tracked. Select one of the groups to be the focus for the rest of the class. Children in the class are asked to suggest things to change in the scene: where the characters are sitting, their body position or their facial expression. This is known as *forum theatre*. Other children can be chosen to stand behind each of the characters, speaking their thoughts.
3. Digital photographs can be taken of any of the drama activities, to be made into a sheet for children to add captions of the characters' thoughts.
4. Alternatively, a *role on the wall* can be made, where an outline of each character is displayed, and children add Post-it captions. Those attached to the inside of the character are their thoughts and feelings, while those around it can describe outward appearance.
5. The drama activities can be followed up with writing in role, where each child chooses one of the four characters and writes about their feelings and observations of their visit to the park, and of what might happen next (see Figures 3.1 and 3.2 for examples).

These techniques can be used with virtually any story. Imagine, for example, the Greek myth of Pandora's box, where the reactions of both Pandora and her husband are explored. This story also gives you the opportunity to use a further drama technique: *conscience alley*,

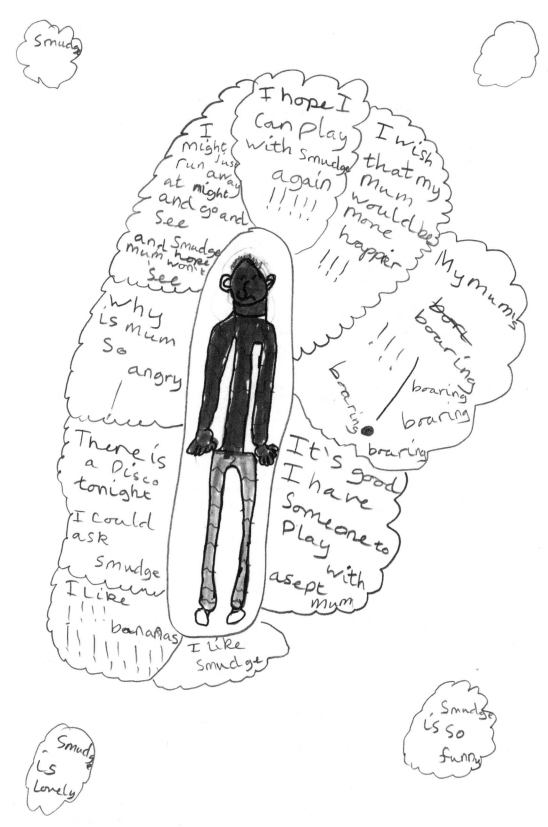

Figure 3.1 A child's writing, following role play using *Voices in the park*

Figure 3.2 A child's writing, following role play using *Voices in the park*: second example

where a child in role as Pandora walks between two facing rows of children, acting as both sides of her conscience. As she walks slowly by them, from one side she hears reasons why she should not open the box, while from the other side she hears temptations to open it. Once at the end of the alley, she must decide what she should do.

Investigating materials

There are many techniques and activities children can try in order to learn how to select appropriate media and tools for future pieces of work (see Box 3.3).

Box 3.3   Art investigations

Investigating paper

Vary the paper that children work on. Try:
- paper circles
- various rectangular strips
- square shapes
- triangular shapes
- ovals
- irregular shapes
- torn paper

made from:
- sugar paper
- newspaper
- art paper
- tissue paper
- card.

What happens when different sizes of paper are used:
- postcards
- rolls of wallpaper
- Post-it notes
- very long, thin strips
- the largest sheets you can find?

Investigating mark making

Ask children to see the different marks they can make with:
- pencils of different grades
- pencil crayons
- wax crayons
- felt-tip pens of different thicknesses
- brushes of different thicknesses used with different types of paint
- one medium layered on to another.

Try making:
- very light marks
- very heavy marks
- a range of marks graded from light to heavy
- hatch marks
- dots of different sizes
- straight, curvy or dotted lines.

As well as working independently, the activities in Box 3.3 can be explored by small groups working around a table. Provide a large sheet of paper of any shape, and either limit the choice of tools or provide a variety from which the children may choose. Ask them to start making any marks they wish on the section of paper that is nearest to them, or ask them to start from a corner, or near to the centre. They can change the types of mark or the tools they are using whenever they wish. After a short time, ask them to move the paper round so that they are looking at the work of their neighbour. Each child continues working, taking the previous work into account. How will they develop it? Repeat this until the paper has come full circle so that each child can see what their own original work has become.

Linking art and music

Try playing different types of music as a stimulus for art. Start by playing the piece to the children, having told them that they will be making some kind of artistic response. Have a variety of materials available so that they can choose to draw, paint or create a collage while the music is played. If you are using a short piece of music, play it several times over the course of the session, but perhaps not constantly. It would be interesting to repeat the exercise several times with different types of music, and ask the children to compare the finished pieces of art. These could be displayed for another class to view while snatches of the musical stimuli are playing to see if they can match the art with the appropriate music.

Art from nature

The environmental artist Andy Goldsworthy uses natural materials to create what are often ephemeral pieces. Goldsworthy uses materials such as petals, pine cones, stones, twigs, grasses – in fact any natural objects that can be safely used without damage to the environment. He very carefully arranges them, sometimes using thorns to pin objects such as leaves together, to create art in the environment. Often the creations take a geometric form, such as a circle made from flower petals, with maybe a centre created from acorns or bark chips. Or perhaps he will build a three-dimensional form from pebbles or sticks. These are left in the environment in which they were found, until they degrade or fall apart naturally. Children will enjoy using the school grounds, or a walk in a nearby park or garden at different times of year, to make their own versions of such creations.

Crossing cultural boundaries

Look at the artistic styles of different cultures, giving children the opportunity to move away from their own cultural expectations. Images or artefacts from, for example, African, Chinese, Native American or Aboriginal Australian cultures all provide stimulating starting points. You could have an Art Workshop day where your room, or the school hall, is set out as though it were a gallery, with artefacts displayed so that they can be viewed from any angle. Provide a wide variety of art resources and allow children to choose both the artefact and the materials with which to represent them.

Write the picture

Using art as a basis for discussion and writing can be another useful device. One example is the work of Marc Chagall, whose paintings suggest dreamlike, fantastic qualities and can lead to much speculation and interpretation. Children could make up their own stories from the paintings which they first tell to a partner and then write as a narrative, choosing their own starting point, perhaps before the frozen moment of the painting, or afterwards, as a recollection. Drama techniques could be used, such as freeze-framing and thought tracking, to further enable the children to consider the motivation and feelings of the characters. As a follow-up, some children may like to paint or draw their own dream interpretations in the style of Chagall, or in a style of their own. For other starting points, look at the the National Gallery's Take One Picture initiative (www. takeonepicture.org), which shows how studying one specific piece of art can lead to interesting creative work in many curriculum areas.

Observational drawing

Observational drawing helps children to focus on what they see rather than what they think they see. Creative artwork requires perceptive visualisation and ever-increasing skills, and the imagination to see everyday things in extraordinary ways. Observation can help with this. Every classroom should have a set of fascinating objects. The teacher can provide these, but it can be good to set the children a challenge to bring objects that will arouse curiosity and perhaps which come with an interesting story.

Don't forget the local environment. Even the mundane motor car could become something more interesting. Don't stop at the outline shapes of the cars; open up the bonnets and draw parts of the engines, or ask for willing members of staff to let the children sit behind the steering wheel and draw a driver's-eye view of the pedals, or the view from the rear-view mirror. Part of such a project could include children's own bikes or scooters, or you may be able to arrange for a much larger vehicle to be brought on to the playground, such as a fire engine, lorry or tractor.

Making music

The musician and conductor Daniel Barenboim, when giving the BBC Reith Lectures of 2006, spoke about the importance of active and concentrated listening to music, including listening to the silence that precedes it. With an understanding of how music is created, using differing degrees of speed, volume and emphasis, as well as the notes themselves, and the juxtaposition of various instruments or body sounds, children can experience the joy of creating music of their own in many different ways. Music is essentially about composing, performing and listening. Creativity is best served by the composition of music. Rehearsal and performance help children to reflect on their compositions. The ability to actively listen is an important part of the whole creative experience. Use every opportunity to engage children with live music of their own and of others.

In groups, or as a whole class, children can create soundscapes to represent different types of machines or weather, or different parts of a poem or story. An important element here is the response and critical comment of peers. In order to help children improve upon their created pieces, the views and opinions of others need to be taken into consideration, while bearing in mind that the original composers do not necessarily have to agree with their critics. In this way, both performers and listeners are developing their musical skills, which will aid their future creativity. The final piece can be an end in itself, or you could use the composition as the basis for a dance piece. Revised and rehearsed pieces can be recorded or performed for others.

Children do not need to be accomplished musicians in order to create music. Both tuned and untuned percussion can be used very effectively, as can computer programs. One starting point is begin with a descriptive poem, or short book. Maurice Sendak's *Where the wild things are* works well here (professionals have also realised the potential, hence an opera and a musical based on the book). Well-chosen stories, poems or picture books can also be used as the basis for interpretative dance. Select a text that has the possibility for a variety of movements, such as a scene from *Ali Baba and the forty thieves*, John Burningham's *Mr Gumpy's outing*, Tony Mitton's *Rumble in the jungle*, Michael Rosen's *We're going on a bear hunt*, or a strongly descriptive poem like Lewis Carroll's 'Jabberwocky' or one with powerful rhythms such as 'Hiawatha'. You can either select appropriate music yourself or at other times ask the children to choose. Break the text up into sections with contrasting interpretations, where perhaps smooth, sinuous movements apply to one section or character, and sharp, jerky movements fit another. Children devise their own sequences of dance moves, which they can reproduce, to fit both music and storyline. This obviously requires several sessions over a period of time in order to produce a complete finished dance that can then be performed.

Sharing the creativity

While it is both commendable and satisfying to create something for its own sake, greater satisfaction and further motivation are gained when the resulting work can be shared with others. Knowing that a performance or a display is going to be the outcome can provide the incentive and context for much of the work children produce. This is, of course, particularly true of the creative arts – art, music and drama – where performance and display are often an intrinsic part of the work. For children to work towards producing something for a known audience gives a tangible context for their efforts, and can result in a genuine pride in the finished product. The concept of 'audience' covers a wide range, from another group within the class, to the full class or another in the school, to another Key Stage or the whole school, and of course parents or guests. Many primary schools, for example, invite local senior citizen groups into school to enjoy performances of musical events that are also shared with other audiences. As we outlined in Chapter 1, if something is creative, then it has to be experienced and evaluated by others.

Science and maths

The creative mind is not static, so harnessing children's innate curiosity and posing interesting problems provides the opportunity for the forward movement necessary for creative thought to flourish. Science is a particularly good area to use to foster creative enquiry in children, as it is essentially about asking questions, forming and solving problems, hypothesising and seeking answers that are open to enquiry and debate from others. Capitalising upon the close links between science and mathematics can help children to be aware of the interdependence of the subjects, where, for example, the answer to a scientific question may require mathematical knowledge and logic. Box 3.4 gives some examples of science challenges of this kind.

Box 3.4   Science challenges

How accurate are local weather forecasts?

Help the children to set up a basic weather station, measuring temperature and rainfall, and noting sunshine, wind, and other types of weather. Compare this with daily weather forecasts from TV or local newspapers.

Can we use the sun to tell the time?

Challenge teams of children to build a sundial that can tell the time as accurately as possible, and is easy to read.

Can you send a fragile object unbroken through the post?

Provide a wide range of materials for teams of children to design and make a package that holds a packet of crisps, or an egg. Send them through the post to the school address, and see how many arrive in good condition.

Who can build the fastest boat?

Set up a course made from a length of guttering balanced on a base and blocked at both ends so that it can contain water. The children must make a model sailing boat from either wood or polystyrene with one single sail made from paper. The challenge is to build the boat that can complete the course in the fastest time, with a hairdryer being used to create the wind force. Calculations of optimum sail area and shape will help to produce the winning vessel.

Science workshop

For a fun and exciting boost to children's enjoyment of science, set up a science workshop in either your classroom or the school hall. This does take some planning, but is well worthwhile and could be a whole-school event. You will need to provide resources and simple written instructions for a variety of science experiments and activities for small groups of children (see Box 3.5 for some examples of activities). Don't forget to have computer-based activities as well. Additional adult help is very useful!

Box 3.5   Science workshop

Magnetic football This board game, which can be bought or made, is a fun way to investigate basic magnetism. The board, which has a football pitch marked on it, is raised on short legs at each corner, to allow players to slide lengths of stick, with magnets attached, underneath in order to move miniature footballers placed on the board, each with a magnet stuck to their base. The aim of the game is obviously to score goals!

Raisin in lemonade When a raisin is placed into lemonade, bubbles of the carbon dioxide in the liquid form on the raisin's rough surface, making it rise to the top, demonstrating that air is lighter than liquids or solids. As the bubbles escape at the surface, so the raisin sinks, and the process begins again.

Monster slime Investigate changing materials by mixing custard powder, green food dye and enough water so that when you touch it, it is a solid, but it can also be poured.

Bottle orchestra Provide a range of glass bottles, jugs, water and wooden beaters; challenge children to create a musical scale.

Helicopters Cut and fold paper to create simple helicopters that twirl when thrown into the air to demonstrate air resistance. What happens if you use different sizes or weights of paper?

Magic balloons Play with static electricity by rubbing inflated balloons against clothing and using it to pick up pieces of tissue paper. Make this into a race – who can transport the greatest number of pieces to the end of a course in a given time?

Kitchen golf Roll golf balls down kitchen-roll tubes to try to get them to stop in certain places, to score points. A fun way to investigate forces.

Rocket science Use balloon pumps to power paper rockets. Whose can go the furthest?

An energy survey

Our influences on the rise of global warming can be investigated by involving the children in an energy survey of the school. This should not only make them aware of how energy is used in the building, but perhaps also cause them to ask questions about their own and their families' uses of energy. They may even come up with some practical solutions. Start by asking pairs or groups of children to measure the temperature changes in different parts of the building and at different times of day. Don't just stick to the classroom. Ask them to suggest which parts of the school to study and why, and how and where the results of their research should be shared. The children will have their own ideas for conducting an energy survey, but they could include such points as where are lights left on? Are radiators sited in energy-efficient places? Are doors and windows left open? Is rubbish sorted for recycling? Is water wasted? Armed with their results, what suggestions might the children have for improvement?

Planning a party – a multi-maths event

Providing a purpose for any work makes it more meaningful, and none could be more so than involving the children in preparations for the end-of-term party, whether it be at Christmas or any other time of year. The important point is that this should be real, not theoretical. So many skills are required that this activity is truly multifaceted, and it may be that different children can be made responsible for different elements. If you begin simply by asking, 'What should we have at our party?', headings will emerge from which working groups can be organised. Likely headings are food, drinks, music and games. Trying to please everybody is a real problem; accommodating likes and dislikes, and taking account of time, space, quantities required and, of course, funding, will all require considerable mathematical skill, co-operation, collaboration and the use of many thinking skills. Your role is as arbiter, invited expert and facilitator, and it is not easy! The results, however, should be worthwhile in more than one sense, not least in helping the children to realise that what they want and what is possible may not be the same!

Shape and space workshop

The workshop idea works as well in maths as in other subjects. A shape theme is an easy one to plan as there is usually a good store of resources available to use. Arrange your work space with various shape-related resources for children to explore, with clearly written instructions where appropriate. Remember that if you are trying to encourage your children to be creative thinkers, using available resources in innovative ways, detailed instructions about what to do may not be helpful, unless of course you then ask them to see what happens if they change something! Here are some ideas:

- Using a limited number of interlocking cubes, how many different ways can you link them together? Can you record this on paper?
- Investigate which regular 2D shapes can be used to create tessellating patterns. Are there any shapes that cannot be used?
- What is the tallest tower you can build using only sheets of A4 paper and sticky tape? What happens if you use larger sheets of paper?
- What is the greatest number of times a piece of paper can be folded in half? Does it change if the size of the paper changes?

Measuring

Set up an investigation to check the sizes of furniture relative to different ages of children.

- Are all rooms equipped to cater for children of different heights?
- Do they have any suggestions to make things better?
- Broaden the children's understanding of what we mean by 'measuring'. As well as having them measure lengths, heights, areas and perimeters both in and outside the classroom, challenge them to devise a method for measuring noise and light levels.

Data handling

As part of a school healthy eating programme, carry out a lunch-box survey leading to the producing of pictograms or bar charts.

- Make a bar chart of the colours of the boxes.
- Carry out a survey of the contents of the lunch boxes. How healthy are they?
- How could the results be shared?
- Do the children form any conclusions or hypotheses that could be tested further?

Results could form the basis for further work to encourage healthier eating, such as designing posters or making presentations to classes.

Another data handling exercise could involve looking at a space with multiple uses such as the hall, asking how much it is used for different purposes and for how long over the course of a week. This will necessitate interpreting timetables and calculating time. As well as asking for results to be presented in particular ways, such as bar or pie charts, ask the children to suggest alternative methods of presentation. Do any conclusions or questions arise from the results?

Starting to extend everyday creativity

Making the most of popular culture

For many children, the worlds of home and school are totally separate, with different and sometimes opposing cultures at work, but this disparity can provide opportunities for the creative practitioner. Using everyday experiences from outside school can motivate and engage children, using their often considerable knowledge as the context for developing essential learning skills.

One way you can make such links is in using the popular ranges of game cards that many children enjoy playing with and trading. Boys in particular often have an amazing store of information on the characters and their various 'powers', understanding the complex rules of play at a high level (for an example of how a child was inspired by Digimon characters to write a book, see *How to help your child read and write* by Dominic Wyse (2007)). Develop language skills by asking the children to share their knowledge through teaching others how to play the games. The knowledge about game cards can be built on by linking with the school curriculum, for example with historical characters. Children can design and make their own character cards, choosing appropriate qualities and powers for specific and generic characters associated with Romans, Victorians, Tudors or ancient Egyptians before going on to develop rules for playing games with them. Using analogy can make for more concrete understanding of the motivations of historical characters, and the reasons for key events.

Theme days

Special focused theme days can raise children's awareness of the world beyond their immediate boundaries, arousing curiosity and awakening interest. A class or, even better, a whole-school theme day based on a particular country or continent is a good way to do this. One school had a 'Europe Day', where the European national anthem, Beethoven's 'Ode to Joy', was played in a whole-school assembly to start the day. Groups of children formed of several from each year group 'visited' different European countries in classrooms across the school, enjoying a variety of activities in each new place. For example:

- In France they played *boules*, role-played in a French market and contributed towards building a model of the Eiffel Tower from rolled up newspaper.
- In Holland they learned a clog dance and tasted Dutch cheese.
- In Greece they ate olives and taramasalata and learned some letters of the Greek alphabet.
- In Spain they used castanets to accompany Spanish dancing.

There was also traditional Scottish and Irish dancing, lots of opportunities to taste foods and try a variety of modern foreign languages as well as looking at PowerPoint loops of images of the countries, including maps and flags. Many other activities were planned by the whole staff, and children had a specially produced 'passport' that was stamped at each country they visited as a reminder of the day to take home and share with their parents, while photographs were taken throughout the day to be published later on the school website.

4 The local environment

There are few things as familiar to a child as their school. An environment with which we are entirely familiar can seem to hold nothing new for us, but looking at it in different ways can open our minds to fresh possibilities. Looking in different ways at the familiar can be an important starting point for creativity. Creative thinking and critical questioning about familiar environments may lead to interesting and innovative solutions. This process is much helped by co-operative working and a teacher acting as an enabler and facilitator rather than a purveyor of knowledge.

In January 2006, the Department for Education and Skills (DfES) published the *Learning outside the classroom manifesto*. The manifesto aims to involve as many agencies as possible in providing learning outside the classroom, stating that 'Every young person should experience the world beyond the classroom as an essential part of learning and personal development, whatever their age, ability or circumstances' (p. 1). The learning outside the classroom they have in mind is 'The use of places other than the classroom for teaching and learning [that provide] memorable learning experiences . . . which affect our behaviour, lifestyle and work . . . and influence our values and the decisions we make' (p. 1).

Figure 4.1 shows which areas of the local environment can be thought about in a creative way.

Classroom swap

Have you ever thought of swapping classrooms to experience working in a different environment? The following are some questions to ask in a classroom swap:

1. What can you see from the place you are now sitting?
2. What things are difficult to see?
3. What can you hear?
4. What does it feel like to sit in this place?
5. What works well about the way this room is organised?
6. What might be changed to make the room work better?
7. What do you like about this room?
8. Is there anything that you don't like? Why?

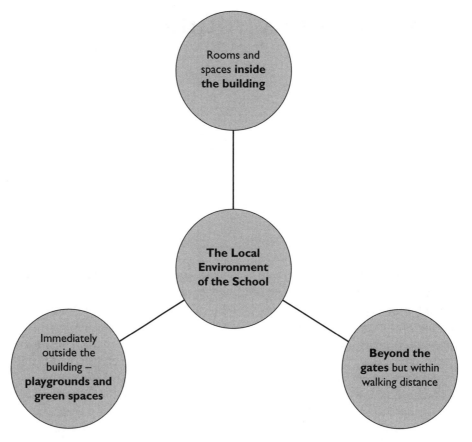

Figure 4.1 The local environment

The questions could be used simply as prompts for a whole-class discussion, or copies of the questions could be given to pairs or small groups of children as a basis for group discussion. In this kind of activity, it can be useful to give individuals in a group specific tasks. For example, one child could read the questions, one could organise the order for children to give answers and see that everyone has a fair chance, one could scribe notes and one could be responsible for feeding back at the end. This avoids everyone talking at once and results in there being a definite outcome. On occasion you might feel that you want to begin with quiet personal reflection. Perhaps the questions could be given to individuals in the form of a simple questionnaire, to be filled in silently before feeding back to a partner, group or the whole class.

Make sure the children realise that there are no right answers to the questions, but where appropriate they should be encouraged to justify their answers by using the word 'because', for example 'I like this room because there're more displays on the wall compared to our room' or 'It's difficult to see the board because the sun is shining on it at the moment.'

Next, give the children an A3-sized basic outline plan of the room, with tables, chairs, board, windows, etc. marked, but with a large margin around the edge. Ask the children to show their position on the plan and, in the margin, annotate it with some of their answers to the questions. Once complete, move everyone to a different place and repeat the exercise. Do they prefer one place in the room to the other? Why? Armed with this information you can now ask the children to redesign the room on another piece of paper. What changes would they make? Depending upon their age and ability, you could introduce concepts such as scale, or present criteria such as the necessity for a particular number of tables and chairs, drawer units, etc. Figures 4.2 and 4.3 show how some children interpreted this task.

While you are busy scrutinising and offering suggestions for changes to someone else's classroom, remember that they will be doing the same thing in yours! The next step is to pair up children from the two classes for them to see and discuss their results. Having the prompt questions as a starter for the conversation could be useful. Following this, each class will have new views and opinions about their own working space to consider, so a new set of questions may be needed to guide the next discussion. The following are some questions to ask after a classroom swap:

1. What did your partner from the other class say about our room?
2. What did you think about what they said?
3. What suggestions did they make about how we might change our room?
4. What do you think about their suggestions?
5. Do you think we should actually make any of the changes?
6. How manageable would the changes be? Might they cause any problems or difficulties?
7. How did you feel about someone being in our room and making suggestions about how we could change it?
8. What did your partner from the other class say or think about your ideas for their room?
9. Has the classroom swap made you look at our room differently?
10. Are there any ideas from the other classroom that you would like to see in our room?

Having had the experience of this activity in a different room, the children will be more objective in their views of their own classroom, so go through the same procedure for your own room. The most important part of the process is to make some changes to the classroom environment and evaluate over time how well they work.

Beyond the classroom

If we step just beyond the classroom to the rest of the school building, there are corridors, cloakrooms, a hall, other classrooms, a library. There are entrances and exits and various routes around the school. There are 'adults only' areas. To begin simply by investigating the purposes and uses of different spaces within the school building can act as a stimulus for many areas of the curriculum, as well as encouraging children to think about the familiar in a new way, to question, and to answer their own questions.

The following are some questions we might ask children about the inside of our school:

1. Who uses this room/space/area?
2. What do they use it for?
3. When do they use it?
4. Could it be used for anything else?

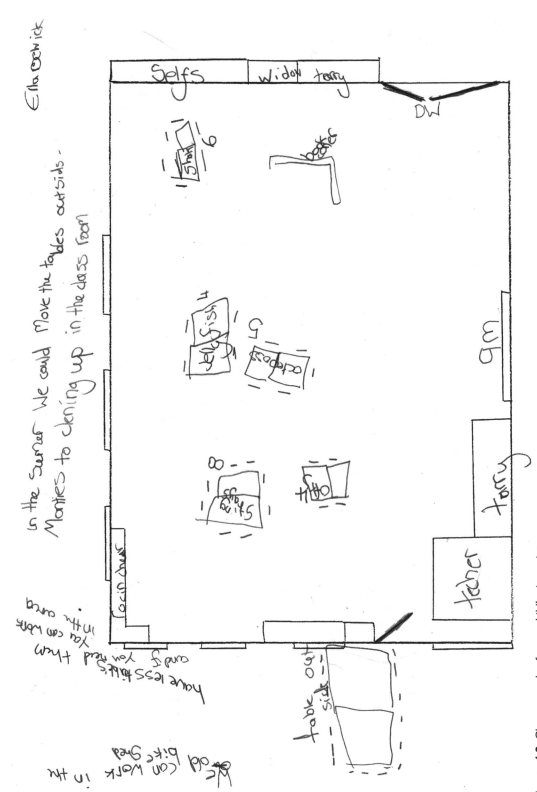

Figure 4.2 Classroom plan from a child's viewpoint

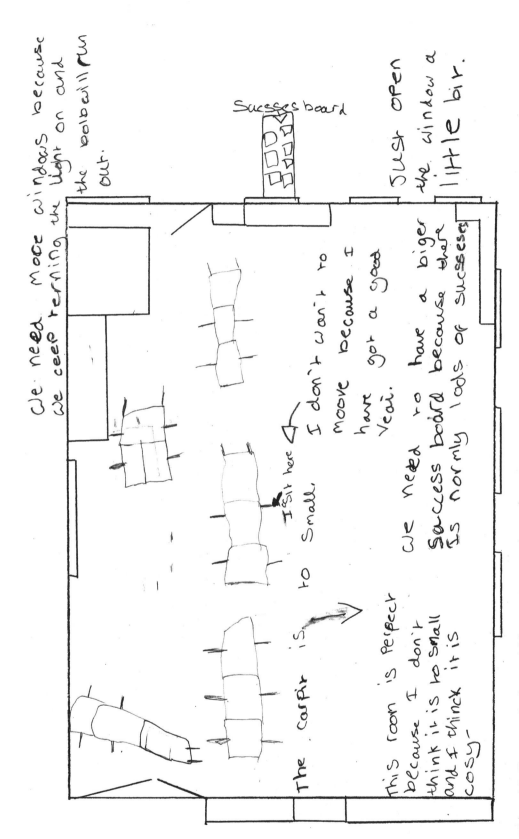

Figure 4.3 Classroom plan from a child's viewpoint: second example

5. What things about this space work well? Why?
6. What things about this space don't work too well? Why?
7. How might it be improved? (Realistically and/or idealistically.)
8. Does the way in which this space is used cause difficulties or problems for anyone else?

What could then be done with the answers? Children could:

*   make their own information books, with drawings, photographs and writing about particular rooms or spaces;
*   make lift-the-flap books, the flaps being photos of the room, together with the question 'Who uses this room?' or 'What is this space in the room used for?' – the answer being hidden under the flap;
*   present their findings in the form of a report, which could be used, together with illustrations, as a display for the whole school to share.
*   take digital photographs of the rooms and spaces, draw and annotate plans, and create 'artist's impressions' to show possible alternatives;
*   plan a display with quotes from some of the answers to the questions, along with the further question 'What do YOU think?' and a blank sheet for comments;
*   publish the report on the school's website;
*   take the findings to a School Council meeting for further discussion.

When the thinking about the school as a whole has been done, it is important that some changes are made, so that the activities have a purposeful outcome.

Playgrounds and green spaces

> [I]f educators recognised school grounds as increasingly important sites for environmental learning, then no matter how limited the potential of the school grounds, they would make decisions that recognise their value as an integral dimension of children's learning.
>
> (Tranter and Malone, 2004, p. 153)

> As soon as we move out of the confines of the school building, we open up endless possibilities for learning and teaching. 'What we see, hear, taste, touch, smell and do gives us six main "pathways to learning". Young people are intensely curious and should be given the opportunity to explore the world around them.'
>
> (DfES, 2006, p. 3)

Take the school playground, for example. As a place where children spend their out-of-class times, playgrounds are frequently uninspiring places. Apart from break times, the main use that most pupils would associate the playground with is PE lessons in good weather. Of course, the best teachers have always been awake to the possibilities of using this outside space more inventively, such as measuring distances in maths, or investigating rainfall, evaporation or shadows in science. But can we use our playgrounds more creatively even than that?

Look back at the set of questions about the inside of the school. They could just as easily be used to find out about the environment outside the school building. Depending on how much your school grounds have been developed, children – and teachers – may well have somewhat fixed views about how the space is used, which could be challenged in order to provoke discussion designed to redefine the possibilities. The national Creative Partnerships initiative included many examples of schools redesigning playgrounds by using the ideas of children and other members of the school community.

Developing walls – a place for drama?

Most schools have blank and boring outside walls that can be transformed into more interesting backdrops, perhaps inspiring dramatic play. Figure 4.4 shows how one school changed its local environment in this way.

Green spaces

For those with the luxury of playing fields or garden space around the school, the move from the man-made environment of the playground to the natural world opens up exciting opportunities. In a country where many children have limited experience of exploring the natural world, their understanding of nature often comes through a screen. Some have argued that this is a kind of 'nature deprivation'. Experiencing first-hand the marvels and miracles of the natural environment is important not only for children's personal and, arguably, spiritual development, but also for the health of the planet. If we do not help our young people to see the value of the natural world, how can we expect them to care about its preservation?

National Curriculum Key Skills and Thinking Skills underpin the following suggestions. These skills are content free, allowing teachers to adapt the ideas to meet the

Figure 4.4 Example of a creative courtyard, with painted, *trompe-l'oeil* images on the walls

requirements of their own classes. The subject headings below provide the main focus for each themed project. The essence of the activities is:

- looking
- listening
- speaking
- thinking
- imagining
- questioning.

The outcomes, however, cannot be prescribed. If we are aiming to encourage our pupils to think and question, they will inevitably begin to travel along unexpected pathways and offer unexpected suggestions. Even when we can see that these suggestions may not work, there is value for the young learner in discovering that for themselves. Risk taking, blind alleys and mistakes are all part of creativity. If our pupils never make mistakes, we could ask why they are in our classrooms at all.

The following ideas, which are designed to give children creative approaches to learning, could be used across the whole year, fitting them into your normal plans by having them provide extensions or different starting points to your usual work. Alternatively, you could use them as one-off tasters into working in slightly different ways. Digital photography, both still and video, could be linked to many of the suggestions and used as a way of recording, displaying and presenting through multimedia.

Science focus

Life processes and living things:

- Study plants of all types and at different times of the year. (Children are not always aware that grass is a plant!) We tend only to use school grounds in this way in summer or perhaps briefly in autumn, but a longer-term project can develop awareness from a different perspective. Seasonal changes can be photographed from the same point of view over the course of the year, with differences being noted.
- Select an appropriate area to set up a vegetable plot. Involving the children in planning what is to be grown, and where, will help to develop their knowledge and understanding about plant growth linked to weather and the seasons. Each class could have its own raised bed; compost bins could be made where children (and staff!) are encouraged to discard their fruit or vegetable snack waste, as well as enlisting the help of the school kitchen. If possible, invest in a water butt and reinforce not only the need for water to grow healthy plants, but also the implications when drought is a feature of the environment. Growing food in this way links very well with the healthy schools agenda and *Every child matters*. It is also an ingredient of becoming an eco-school, linked closely to education for sustainable development.
- Investigate the habitats for 'minibeasts', birds and small mammals in the grounds. Why do we see some creatures at certain times? How does weather affect what we can find? How could we improve the environment to encourage more animals to live here? How might we affect the creatures around us? Draw up a list of rules for animal watching. One school created a 'butterfly garden', selecting plants to attract more

butterflies. They also put up ladybird boxes and made log piles to encourage other insects.

- Set up a project for the children to design a nature trail around as many different areas as possible. Observation and question points could be set up along the trail, using the senses as starting points. What can you see? Hear? Smell? What do the plants feel like here? (As a health and safety rule, of course, this is an opportunity to warn against using the sense of taste in these circumstances!)

- Use the annual BBC *Spring Watch* and *Autumn Watch* campaigns to encourage the children to get closer to nature. Being seasonal, these programmes can provide the stimulus for similar observations in the local environment. You could set up your own school spring or autumn watch projects. Nesting boxes and feeding stations could be sited at various points around the grounds, with the children suggesting where these might be, on the basis of research and questioning. One school also set up a web camera in the nesting box so that children could watch the events unfold on a continuous basis.

- Try birdwatching from the classroom window. Create a classroom 'hide' by masking the windows with black sugar paper, leaving a viewing slot at the appropriate height. Children can generate their own ways of recording the birds they see, having first considered how they could encourage birds to come close enough to be observed, as well as how they will recognise the different species. If your classroom does not lend itself to this activity, where else in school might it be possible? Ask the children to suggest and test locations.

- Set up a weather-watching programme in which children can record as many elements of the weather as you wish, from simply noting whether days are mostly sunny, rainy, cloudy, etc. to measuring wind speed or rainfall. The findings could be compared to the previous day's television or newspaper predictions as well as to internet weather sites, to test accuracy. A nice link could be made with the modern foreign language that is being learned in your school, with the week's weather-watchers displaying their findings in that language as well as English, or indeed in any home languages that may be used by other pupils.

Materials and their properties:

- Plan and create an outdoor science area. Building opportunities for play with a wide variety of materials such as water, soil, rocks, sand, pebbles, gravel, clay, etc. can enable children to ask their own questions and pose their own problems as well as discover the properties of the materials, their similarities and differences. If possible, provide pumps, tubes, paddle wheels, etc. Storage will need to be considered, of course – what solutions can the children suggest? Can they predict what effects the weather might have? What health and safety rules do they think there should be?

Physical processes:

- Use playground equipment to investigate forces and energy, where pushes and pulls are necessary to have fun!

- Observe the effects of sunlight outside, how the sun appears to move across the sky and where shadows fall. Measure the lengths of the shadows throughout the day, marking them with chalk at timed intervals. Make simple sundials and decide where the best place to put them would be. Test them out and see whether you need to make any changes.

- Build an area for experimenting with sound. How far can various sounds travel? What materials work best for creating sound outdoors? What natural materials can be used to create sounds? Link with music by creating 'natural' percussion instruments, such as suspending lengths of wood or slate on string to be struck with a variety of beaters. Can you make the sounds high or low, loud or quiet? How can you change or stop sounds? Record them. Can others guess what made the sounds? You could record a sound trail around the grounds.

History focus

- Whatever their age, make use of the school buildings. Look at building styles and how they reflect their historical period. In what ways does the school building match other local buildings? If the building has been altered or extended, what clues can be seen to show this? Are there any plaques or date stones? What information does this give you about the way the building has been used in the past? If you have access to old school log books, is there any extra information that can be added to what you can see for yourself? If the building is very new, what information could it provide for future historians? What would they learn about how the school is used now? Get the children to design their ideal school.
- Make your own archaeological area. Choose a piece of ground to excavate by measuring and digging a trench, noting anything that you find. Obviously, this may yield nothing at all, but if you go down more than a few inches, you could discover layers of soil changing. However, your main purpose will be to create a pseudo-dig in which children can select and bury a variety of artefacts that will be left for various periods of time before being dug up again to investigate what has happened to them. In this way, children can develop an understanding not only of the way in which archaeologists work, but also of what materials can survive underground and what will rot away, thereby creating puzzles for archaeologists to solve. Looking at what is *not* there is sometimes as important as looking at what is!

Geography focus

- Use compasses to find where the points of the compass are in your outside classroom. Chalk or paint them on to the playground. These could be used when studying the apparent movement of the sun across the sky.
- Make plans and maps of the outside area, labelling and annotating as appropriate. These could be drawn to scale for older pupils.
- Plan routes around the grounds, using either compass directions or non-standard measurements, in conjunction with maps or plans. Can other children follow your route?

Art focus

- Make sure each child has a personal sketch book and encourage them to create their own drawing frequently. From time to time, encourage them to develop their best idea in a different format.
- There are almost limitless possibilities for observational work, either drawn, painted or photographed. These observations can be used as ends in themselves or be added to art sketchbooks or portfolios as resources for later use. Don't neglect the study of colour in observation, where children can try to mix paints to match those in nature.
- Emulate the wonderful art of Andy Goldsworthy by using natural found materials to create environmental pieces. Some of these may last for some time but most are likely to be short-lived and therefore appreciated in a different way. It is worth photographing these ephemeral pieces.
- Three-dimensional work can quite literally offer a different dimension. Try creating sculptures using wire frames and Modroc in the style of Modigliani. Modigliani is perhaps better known as a painter than as a sculptor, his portraits being recognisable by his simplified and elongated style. He used the same basis for his sculptures of people, which are characterised by their tall, thin bodies with very little detail. Not only can these be made outdoors, but, if treated, they can stay outdoors for some considerable time.
- Emulate the Impressionists! Work outside to capture the feel and movement of light, clouds, changing colours. Try chalking on the playground.
- Use the theme of Entrances and Exits to collect images of windows and doors. These could be photographed or drawn as the basis for collages in various forms.
- A longer-term project could be to develop a school sculpture trail. Working in wood or stone, children could make sculptures around a selected theme to be positioned around the grounds. One school invested in an artist-in-residence, who used a chainsaw to make wooden sculptures of animals. The children not only were able to see the artist at work (from a safe distance!), but also were inspired to make their own wooden pieces, and can now enjoy the finished pieces in their outdoor space.
- Make tunnels, domes or barriers using willow weaving. Using this technique, single willow cuttings, once stuck into the ground and kept well watered, root easily and will grow into complete structures if the very pliant stems are woven into shapes. If you can source cuttings yourself, keep them in water for a few weeks in early spring before planting. Alternatively, they can be bought in bulk from specialist firms. Children can plan what to make with the willows and will certainly be needed to keep them well watered while they establish themselves (worth considering when choosing where to position your willows, or there could be a very long walk with watering cans!).
- Make totem poles. These can be temporary structures made from cardboard boxes fixed on top of each other, or more permanent features made from wood or Modroc. Animals could be the theme, or other images more suited to your own school.
- Create a pebble mosaic in which each child paints a pebble before they are set into concrete. Alternatively, leave the stones in their natural state, making the chosen design using just the gradations of colour within the stones themselves.

Maths focus

- Look for 2D and 3D shapes in the school buildings and play equipment. Draw or photograph them for use in displays. What examples can you find of reflective, rotational or translational symmetry? What types of angles can be found? Can you see why right angles are important? Models could be made of parts of the building, or the lines and shapes used in an abstract way as the basis for a painting or collage.
- Paint sequences of colour on school garden fences to help children identify pattern and sequencing.
- Extend your maths trail to include the school grounds as well as the buildings and playground.
- Make frequency tables, for example by counting the number of specific plants in a certain-sized square or a hoop.

PSHE focus

- Involve the children in developing an area of the grounds for quiet contemplation; not every child wants to run around every playtime. Having a special area set aside for reflection or quiet conversation can help children develop a deeper appreciation of the natural world and the pleasure of being outdoors. Choosing aromatic plants is a good idea for such spaces as well as those with flowers or interesting foliage. Places to sit are also important, as are agreed rules for the use of the space.

PE focus

- Use orienteering as a purposeful way of guiding children around the school grounds. This links to geography and also PSHE through teamwork. It does need some setting up beforehand, but once ideas have been trialled, children could work together to plan their own courses for others to follow.
- Create a fitness trail, or even several, each one taking a different route around the grounds. At certain points, provide particular activities to be done such as step-ups on to suitable raised surfaces, star jumps, press-ups, or particular exercises using your own playground equipment.

Literacy/drama focus

- Write descriptions, using virtually anything outdoors as your stimulus. Use a variety of viewpoints, from close-up and minute to looking at the big picture. Or try starting big and 'zooming in' to the specific. The senses really come into play here, with children using all of them to create a description, or indeed limiting themselves to just one selected sense. The outcome could be purely narrative or in poetic form.
- Use areas of your environment as settings for stories. Children could create a story map showing where different parts of their story take place. Finished stories could have illustrations of the settings, either drawn or photographed.
- Create a story garden with simple seating and a special story chair.

- Put up a child-sized story tent where groups can share books or oral storytelling. Perhaps children could gather together artefacts to place in the tent as a stimulus for stories. Each new week could have new objects to generate a new range of stories!

If you have any doubts about whether it is worthwhile considering developing the use of the school grounds, take a look at the following data from Learning Through Landscapes, the national school grounds charity founded in 1990. In 2003, it commissioned a questionnaire of over 350 schools across the country who had improved their school grounds in some way. The findings were that:

- 83 per cent said that that it improved the quality of play;
- 52 per cent reported that it reduced the amount of time taken to settle back into work after break times;
- 65 per cent noted improved attitudes to learning;
- 52 per cent said there was improved academic achievement;
- 64 per cent commented that it reduced the amount of playtime incidents of bullying;
- 65 per cent had increased the number of lessons taught outside;
- 84 per cent felt that there had been improved social interaction.

(Learning Through Landscapes, 2003)

Further afield

No two schools are alike, nor are their locations, so moving outside into the immediate environment – that within walking distance – will obviously provide a wide range of possibilities, depending upon the locality. However, there are some common themes that can be adapted for use in most situations. Having a particular focus or theme in mind as a starting point will direct your initial thinking at the planning stage and help to define your learning intentions. When planning, remember the key elements:

- looking
- listening
- speaking
- thinking
- imagining
- questioning.

Buildings in the local environment – a historical theme

While the basis for this theme springs from a historical context, it is important to bear in mind that what follows incorporates a cross-curricular approach that includes elements of speaking and listening, reading, writing, geography, science, religious education, art and ICT, and covers many key learning and thinking skills.

Religious buildings such as temples, churches, mosques and synagogues can provide a wealth of opportunities for learning, and fortunately are within walking distance of most schools. The following suggestions are based on using a parish church, although most activities would work equally well with any other notable building that you have access to.

We tend to classify buildings by their use. With this notion in mind, you could begin by showing the class images of a number of different buildings that they are unlikely to be familiar with and ask them what they think the buildings are used for, ranging from homes of various types to banks, shops, offices, factories, museums, hospitals, hotels, cafés, stately homes, etc. Ask the children how they work out what the buildings are used for. Finish with the building you are about to use as the basis for your forthcoming work, which of course the children are likely to recognise. As with the earlier work on looking at the school building and the rooms and spaces in it, here we want the children to take a fresh view of the building itself as a historical resource – as an enormous and valuable piece of evidence, and not just as a place of worship. Old buildings are like time capsules, full of artefacts and clues about life in the past: the people, the community, reflections of the wider world. So, make your pupils *time detectives* with the job of discovering all they can, with the building as their starting point. Motivation is a powerful learning tool, so your own enthusiasm in introducing the project should be linked to what the children are likely to be interested in. If the thought of a long history project would be the last thing some of your pupils would warm to, the way in which you present it to them is crucial. The idea of time detectives usually works well, as does the use of ICT for research and presentation.

When visiting the building, ask the children to 'travel back in time', blotting out the twenty-first century around them as much as they can. Ask them to imagine walking out of the main entrance to the building and seeing *not* what is there now, but what was there twenty, a hundred, two hundred, five hundred years ago. What would they have seen and heard? What from today might have been there then? Any of the current buildings or trees? Would they have looked the same? What would people have been wearing? How would they have been travelling? What would their homes have been like? What food would they have eaten? How would they have spent their time? What modern things would they *not* have known about?

Organising the work

It is essential that you have made exploratory visits yourself to the building you are going to use, and that you have gained information yourself on its history. This is not because you are going to take on the role of official guide; far from it, but having background knowledge helps you to plan the work efficiently and effectively.

You need to decide whether you want all the children to work on everything, or whether the class is to be divided into groups who will focus on particular elements, which will then be fed back to the whole class. The group method has much to commend it:

- It mirrors the way teams work in the real world.
- It encourages co-operative, collaborative working.
- It allows in-depth study and the development of individual 'expertise' in one area.
- It provides a real audience for the final work.
- It offers pupils the chance to develop their skills in providing critical feedback.
- It provides opportunities for re-presenting work in the light of feedback, or for further development based on unexpected questions.
- It is efficient use of time when visiting the building.

Mixed-ability groups work best in this kind of situation, perhaps using the idea of assigning particular roles to individuals, as has been previously suggested. Groups could be organised to focus on particular aspects such as:

- the building from the outside;
- the area around the building;
- separate sections of the inside of the building.

When the children visit the building they become time detectives searching for clues and evidence. Table 4.1 might be used to focus their investigations.

Discuss with the children ways of finding the necessary evidence or clues. These will include close observation, making notes and drawings, taking photographs (after seeking relevant permission) and possibly conducting interviews, for example with a religious leader associated with the building or anyone who uses it regularly for a variety of purposes such as a choir member, worshipper or helper. Children can make rubbings of old brasses, inscriptions, etc., or make annotated plans of sections of the building. Useful information can also be gathered from any existing guidebooks, but this perhaps should be kept until after the children have had the chance to form their own opinions.

When the children are investigating the area around the building, there is a chance that more evidence will be found, especially if there are memorial inscriptions providing primary evidence about individual people. There may be buildings nearby that have links with the main building being studied, such as community rooms or almshouses. Children can read noticeboards to find clues about how the building is currently used or

Table 4.1 *Time detectives*

Time Detectives

Complete as much of this evidence sheet as you can. Further investigation may be needed for some areas. You have to find out as much as possible about the building.

Agent:	Location: Exterior	Date:
	Evidence/Clues	**Possible conclusions**
What materials have been used in the building, and for what purposes?		
What is the age of the building?		
Why was it built in this location?		
What tools were used to make the building?		
What skills were needed to make the building?		
How long did it take to build?		
What is the building used for?		
Are there any unusual or special features?		

associations it has with local groups. They could also look at any plants and trees near the building and work out why they are there. Are they for decorative purposes or do they have other significance? They should also be on the lookout for anything unusual or interesting that may require further investigation. It is a good idea to encourage children to devise their own questions following their observations. Ask them, 'What else do you want or need to know?' as a starting point for their follow-up research.

Once you are inside the building, its particular use will determine to some extent what can be discovered, but the following starting points could provide the focus for groups to investigate:

- Is there more than one entrance to the building? Why might this be?
- Where are the windows positioned? Are they high up or low down? Why is that? Is there anything special about the windows? Why might that be?
- What materials have been used in making the building? Where do you think they might have come from?
- What special skills would have been needed to make the building and the objects inside it?
- What is the sound like inside the building? Does it make you feel that you have to be quiet? Does it echo? Why might that be?
- How is the building furnished? How is the seating arranged? Why is it arranged in that way? What clues does this give you about how the building is used?
- Is the roof unusual? In what way?
- Are there any objects with writing on? What information are they giving you? Why have they been displayed for everyone to read? How old are they?
- Are there any special or unusual things in the building? Can you work out what they are used for?
- Do you have any questions about the inside of the building?
- Does music play a role in the use of the building? What evidence can you find for this?

It is, of course, also worth looking at the current use of the building, perhaps comparing this to ways in which it has been used in the past.

Of course, gathering this wealth of information is not necessarily an end in itself. Armed with a new body of knowledge and some unanswered questions of their own, your time detectives now have to piece together their evidence and clues in order to see what further investigation they may have to undertake back in school. This can be done through the use of the internet, local histories or guidebooks to the building, by looking at old photographs, by accessing parish records or census returns, or through interviews with local residents. In this way, children are gathering historical information from both primary and secondary sources.

Final products from the project might be a large-scale wall display showing annotated photographs from each group's investigations, together with paintings, drawings or collages of people from the past who used the building in some way, based on the children's imaginary journeys and linked to research about clothing and occupations.

From their experiences, children could write in role, perhaps as one of the original builders, or as one of the real people who have used the building in the past for any number of reasons. The writing could take the form of autobiographies, reports, diaries or poems. Incidents, either real or imagined, could be recreated in dramatic form and presented to other classes, or parents. A children's version of a guide to the building could be produced, including photographs the children have taken, or scanned images of artwork, together with their own information from their research. A video guide could be made, including interesting facts from the research, or a similar presentation made to the school, parents, or an invited audience from the community. Information from inscriptions they have previously found could be brought into this imaginary journey, with names of real people being added to fuel the imagination.

In this example of using the environment outside the school as a stimulus, the work is cross-curricular, based on a real building, involves hands-on activities and requires problem solving. All these features can enable children to think in diverse ways as a part of their curriculum.

5 Creative partnerships

Developing working relationships with other professionals will broaden and enrich your teaching and, consequently, your pupils' learning. In particular, working with people who work in creative fields is likely to enhance the creativity of your pupils and the creativity of your teaching. The title of this chapter was chosen because we think that partnerships of this kind are particularly beneficial. It is of course also the title of the national initiative, which we covered in Chapter 1 and which was built on the idea of partnerships to enhance creative learning.

In 2005, Creative Partnerships published *Building creative futures*, detailing the many successful partnerships that had been forged as part of the initiative. One of the key findings that emerged about pupil learning was the impact of a personalised approach, 'where pupils were given some responsibility for the creative processes and outcomes of their work' (p. 13). Challenge, creative engagement, connecting and reflecting were cited as vital elements.

Working with other schools

With the increased development of local school networks, there are greater opportunities for schools to establish partnerships. Such networks enable expertise and resources to be shared, at the same time as opening up possibilities for creative engagement. Some schools share teaching expertise or loan each other resources or equipment, while others involve the children in working in each other's schools. Obviously, the ease of getting to other schools will determine whether this is an option for you, and is certainly the most challenging choice from a planning point of view, but is probably the most rewarding.

Creative arts project

Two Suffolk schools combined on a major creative arts project that became an annual event. Teachers, teaching assistants and children, as well as the county advisory teacher for dance and a drama teacher from the local upper school, worked in each other's schools. Each year, a musical theme formed the basis for a range of activities, which included dance, drama, music, art and literacy. Planning started early in the year; all the adults involved chose the area in which they preferred to work and selected the activities they would plan and deliver. Well-known musicals were used for the songs that were learned in each school before the actual creative arts week itself took place. These musicals included *Oliver*, *Cats* and a combination of *The Jungle Book* and *The Lion King*, which they renamed *The Jungle King*. The final performance involved all children singing together as well as sharing the dance and drama they had created.

During the week itself, children could select from a programme of options that included such activities as:

- painting backdrops for the performance;
- devising dance pieces based on the theme;
- creating pieces of drama based on the stories;
- making a wide range of associated pieces of art such as masks, animal print collages and Victorian artefacts;
- making props;
- creating lift-the-flap books for younger children;
- composing accompaniments for the songs, to be used in the final performance.

Another example of local school links featured Pam Dowson's school (St Mary's Primary School, Mildenhall), which used the video link facilities at the local college of technology to share investigative maths tasks with a school in Yorkshire. The same schools paired children in Year 12 with those in Year 4. The older pupils discussed the kinds of books the younger pupils might be interested in and then designed and made them.

Learning walks

To stimulate your own thinking, organise a series of 'learning walks' where staff visit each other's schools, either during or after normal school hours, in order to share good practice and swap ideas. Seeing interesting displays and engaging in professional dialogue with colleagues can provide starting points for your own teaching.

Swapping classes

We tend to teach our own classes in our own classrooms, but why not arrange to swap your talents with others in your own school or beyond, by planning to use your own expertise in a colleague's class? For example, perhaps you have a passion for music that you could share with a colleague whose specialism is investigative science, or maybe you could swap your art skills for someone else's dance expertise. Whatever the exchange, everyone benefits (see Chapter 4 for another kind of classroom swap).

Making links with secondary schools that have active drama departments can be another way of developing creative partnerships from which all parties can benefit. Select a theme – it could be anything from jungles to friendships; fairgrounds to conflict – and invite the older students to work with your younger pupils in developing their dramatic skills – in creating a piece of drama that may include dialogue, movement, dance or music. And don't forget that most local authorities have advisory staff with whom you can forge a partnership. Inviting them to help you to enhance your pupils' skills will simultaneously provide you with valuable professional development opportunities.

Links between schools, museums and galleries

The relationship you develop with a museum will depend upon several factors:

- your distance from the museum;
- costs involved in visiting the museum;
- the purposes and curriculum links you wish to support;
- the willingness of the museum staff to be involved;
- what the museum has to offer.

Fortunately, the final two points are unlikely to be problematic. The majority of museums are only too keen to work collaboratively with schools, and even the smallest volunteer-run museum will have enormous possibilities. The Museums, Libraries and Archives Council (www.mla.gov.uk) is the lead strategic agency for museums, libraries and archives. It is sponsored by the Department for Culture, Media and Sport, and works with nine regional agencies, which are very active in promoting links with schools, the more imaginative the better.

Making a start

Visit your chosen museum in order not only to familiarise yourself with what it has to offer, but also to see it from a child's viewpoint. Children are often more interested in the building itself rather than the exhibits. Understanding the purposes and designs of museums can be valuable. Could you use them as a context for learning? For example, a Year 4 class visiting Cambridge's Fitzwilliam Museum were fascinated by the glass-sided lift that took them to the basement to hang up their coats, and stunned by the spectacular building, which emulates ancient Greek buildings typified by the Acropolis in Athens (Liverpool's St George's Hall is another good example). Discussions can be prompted about the designs of the external features and internal features of the museum even before consideration of the artefacts inside.

Museums often have well-planned packages available based on knowledge and information sharing about displays and artefacts in the museum collections. This may well be a good starting point, where you begin to get to know both the museum and the staff, but from here you can start to use the museum more creatively. Instead of linking visits to more obvious historic, scientific or art-related content-led topics, try working from an enquiry or skills development basis where children are challenged to work at deeper levels and have the opportunity to enhance particular skills. Here is where working collaboratively with the museum becomes a real partnership. It is a good idea to have an outline proposal of the suggested work to form a basis for dialogue with museum staff, enlisting their support and help. Table 5.1 shows one example.

Table 5.1 *Museum visit planning format*

Museum visit planning	
Learning context	
What I want the children to learn	
What I want the children to do	
What needs to be done before the visit – for the teacher	
What needs to be done before the visit – for the children	

- When and why the Romans invaded Britain.
- What their life was like when they were here.
- Local examples; particularly the story about finding the Mildenhall treasure.

- Ask museum staff questions about the Roman occupation locally, and particularly about the finding of the treasure.
- Look at the replica of the treasure; draw and perhaps photograph it.
- Appraise the way the treasure is displayed to decide how user-friendly it is for children.

- Visit the museum myself and speak to museum staff about the plan.
- Ask whether it is possible to take photographs.
- Arrange date and time of visit.
- Find out about required number of adult helpers, and group sizes.

- Introduce the topic.
- Read Roald Dahl's story *The Mildenhall treasure*, recounting how the treasure was found and what subsequently happened to it.
- Ask children what questions they have about the treasure that may be answered by a visit to the museum.
- Show photographs of the treasure.

Drama and writing in the museum

Portraits and artefacts in museum collections can be used to develop drama and writing skills. One teacher planned alongside the museum education officer of Gainsborough's House museum in Sudbury, Suffolk, where children looked closely at original Gainsborough portraits as the basis for their work.

Some of the planned activities:

- Each child selected a portrait from those on display, and assumed the stance of the sitters, effectively becoming a living portrait. Digital photographs were taken of them – the modern equivalent of the painted portrait. The children were asked to walk as they felt the sitter would have walked. Instinctively they held themselves very erect, chins up, and walked with a measured step. They were then asked to greet each other in an appropriate way, which resulted in 'Good day' or 'Good morning' or 'How do you do?' together with the shaking of hands, or a nod of greeting. From this, short in-role conversations were developed.
- Conversations were also created between the sitter and the artist. Pairs of children created a freeze-frame of the portrait being painted, and were encouraged to imagine the sitter's and artist's thoughts; and to think about what topics might have been

discussed during the sitting. They were also asked to imagine how the sitter might have felt about the finished portrait, and what they might have then said to Mr Gainsborough when the portrait was delivered.

- Following the drama, the children were offered just enough information to help them use their imaginations. They went on to write in role, with the title 'The Portrait Speaks', where the sitter wrote about aspects of their life, or about the day the portrait was painted.
- In 'The Portrait Comes to Life', the children imagined what the sitters' views and questions might be if they were to step out of the portrait, having come to life in the twenty-first century. What changes would they notice? What would surprise them the most? How would they feel about what they saw and heard? How could we explain our lives to them?

Artefacts such as pieces of pottery can be used in a similar way. Children could be asked to imagine who might have made the pot, to imagine their working day and recreate it. Who else might have been around when the pot was made, and what might they have talked about together? Who might have owned the pot? Children could improvise a conversation between the owner and someone else at a time when the pot was in use.

In these examples the children use close observations, speaking and listening skills, dramatic interpretation, imagination and thinking skills to create their own version of a snapshot of someone's life. They are not merely receivers of historical information but creators of factually based scenarios which require deep levels of engagement that will lead to greater understanding not only of the historical contexts, but also about the human condition. As well as having a realistic purpose with a definite conclusion, such a set of activities helps to broaden the children's perceptions of museums, artefacts and portraiture, providing a context in which they can wonder, learn and ask questions as a basis for creating something of their own.

Another collaboration resulted in a term's project where children, working in role as museum designers, were set the challenge of looking critically at one section of their local museum with the task of redesigning it in a more child-friendly way. This involved a considerable number of skills, including evaluation, questioning, problem solving, collaboration, researching, planning and designing as well as subject-based skills in reading, writing, maths, history and art. Their final suggestions were put together as a display in school, which other children appraised, providing helpful responses and feedback, before a special temporary exhibition was mounted in the museum itself.

Developing the partnership

Once you have made a successful link to a local museum, you could take the partnership a step further by planning a year's programme in which termly visits are made to the museum, or the museum staff come to school as part of their outreach work, covering different elements of your teaching programme – encouraging research or questioning skills, for example, or supporting historical investigation, or the development of particular art or technology skills.

Theatre groups

In this book, we emphasise the importance of children experiencing drama themselves in a variety of roles. However, the opportunity to see professional actors at work can also be particularly enjoyable and stimulating. Live theatre extends children's knowledge and appreciation of drama as an art form and can enhance their understanding not only of plots and characters, but also of some of the fundamental aspects of human motivation and interaction. Visits to theatres are expensive, and while they are to be encouraged, it is usually more practical to use travelling theatre groups that specialise in working in schools. While this is not a new idea, such visits are often not used to their fullest potential. What you do before and after performances can offer opportunities that are often overlooked. Bearing in mind the ideas of creative engagement and reflection cited earlier, here are some suggestions for capitalising on theatre group visits.

It is important to give the children a context for the performance so that they do not go into it completely cold; this initial connection will set the scene for the learning that follows, and will depend upon the nature of the performance. Some theatre groups offer the option for groups of children to experience workshops prior to the final performance, in which they then take an active role. Where this is not possible, try asking the children to look for examples of effective drama techniques with which they are familiar, such as the use of props, voice, costume, scenery, sound effects and lighting. This can inform reflective discussions afterwards and lead into their own future dramatic interpretations.

Key questions after the performance include: What did they think worked well? How might they have portrayed elements of the story differently? The children could select small scenes to enact in their own ways, showing similarities and differences from the professional performance for their peers to comment upon. If you approach the theatre group beforehand and explain that this is what you intend to do as a follow-up, they may be prepared to appraise videos of the children's performances, thereby enhancing the whole experience.

Author visits

Meeting a 'real author' can be a truly memorable experience – even a transformative one for some children. This is a point not lost on the Qualifications and Curriculum Authority (QCA), which said, 'We believe that working with a writer is a unique way for children and young people to understand the power of the written word and the excitement of creative composition' (Booktrust, n.d., p. 2).

Prior contact with the author will help to establish your working relationship and make the most of the visit. Give the author basic information about the school and the particular children with whom they will be working; tell them how much the children already know about their work and ask if there is anything the author would recommend you to do as preparation with the children. Establish the main purpose for the visit and discuss what the children will do as follow-up work, asking if the author would be prepared to respond to any work the children produce.

Some authors have excellent websites that the children can access prior to the visit, and some even respond personally to e-mails from young readers. It is best if the children know something of the author's works before the visit as it will then have more impact, as well as enabling them to prepare questions beforehand. If the children already know that they will be doing some follow-up work and the form it will be taking, their questions and observations can feed directly into subsequent activities so that there is real creative engagement with the experience.

To find possible authors, try the following websites. From the Society of Authors – www.societyofauthors.net – comes a helpful guide to organising an author visit. The society's website also has a writer search facility. The Booktrust website, www.book trust.org.uk/writingtogether, provides a well-presented argument for having writers in schools. A QCA-endorsed initiative, it is supported by top writers, who give their reasons for being involved. It also explains how to organise and manage an author visit, covering planning, running and following up. It covers funding, and there is a useful list of contacts.

After the visit

Follow-up activities link three areas:

- **adopt:** children will base their own work on the style, range of content or use of language of the visiting author;
- **adapt:** they will be encouraged to change and adapt it in their own ways;
- **innovate:** their finished product may include additions or extensions and will be their own created outcome.

Such an approach allows children to have that vital responsibility for their own work while providing a helpful structure. Examples of activities include:

- making their own picture book, poem, short story or chapter in the style of the visiting author;
- changing the form, for example writing a poem based on the theme of the author's non-fiction work, or writing a story based on one of the author's poems;
- composing a piece of music linked to the author's work, for example by transforming a poem into a song, or creating a representative piece describing setting or character;
- creating a web page of the author's biographical and bibliographic details;
- designing a poster to publicise the author's books;
- creating a database of similar works for others to search.

Libraries

Librarians not only provide access to the creative world of books, but also can offer much useful advice that will ultimately enable your pupils to use the school library effectively. Developing working partnerships with specialist professionals such as your local librarian or the Schools Library Service (SLS) will prove beneficial. Libraries can provide the information children may need as a basis for their own creative engagement and innovation. Without effective library skills, they will be unable to use the library to its best advantage, and they will lose the potential to discover fictionalised worlds created by others, which of course serve as models for their own imagination and writing. Box 5.1 has some suggestions for library-based activities.

Box 5.1   Library ideas

- Create age-appropriate themed book quizzes, e.g.
  - on a particular non-fiction topic with broad appeal, such as animals, dinosaurs, machines, people in history;
  - about a particular author, including completing book titles, or finding the main characters from named stories;
  - around a genre, such as traditional tales, nursery rhymes, adventure stories, fantasy stories or family stories; but bear in mind that the children will also need to know the answers, and plan how to organise the quiz, including how to reward the winners.
- Devise a questionnaire to find out the opinions about the library of others in their class or the rest of the school, following this up by making suggestions for changes to layout, usage or stock.
- Find out about the reading interests of another child in the school or class, then try to choose books to share with them that they will like.
- Create their own displays in the library, linked to particular authors, genres or themes.
- Take part in the annual national initiative called The Reading Game, which keeps children reading through the summer holidays. Any child who successfully completes the challenge to read six books of their choice receives a certificate and medal.
- Help with topic planning by suggesting possible contents of Schools Library Service topic loan boxes.

If your local library is within walking distance, arrange regular visits for your class so that they can have access to a greater number of books, and learn how the library classification system works. If your school library is not organised in the same way, enlist the help of the librarian to find ways of overcoming this. Help the children learn how to use the electronic search systems that most public libraries now have, in order to develop their research skills. Do let parents and carers know about the links you are making with the local library, and encourage them to enrol their child (or the whole family!) as members, so that learning and the enjoyment of books can continue beyond the school day.

Artists in residence

Working alongside a skilled artist or craftsperson not only acts as a model for developing particular skills, but can provide the motivation for children to create their own works of art. Engaging the help of professional artists is only one way in which you can provide children with this sort of creative partnership; there may well be talented parents, teaching assistants, governors, community members, local art organisations or students at local high schools who may be happy to be involved. Your own art interests or skills could also be valuable, and not just to the children in your class.

Try to ensure an interesting balance of art and craft in your longer-term planning, so that many areas are covered. That way you will be providing opportunities for harnessing children's own many interests and skills, or even jump-starting new ones.

Over the course of a year in one primary school, visiting projects included:

- A wood sculptor who used chainsaws to create pieces destined for a sculpture trail in the school grounds. Children later used a more usual range of child-friendly tools to make their own 3D wooden pieces.
- Felt making, where artists worked alongside children, using unspun wool and dyes to create large felt flowers that were pinned to tree trunk sections and used to decorate the school garden.
- Batik, where large groups worked to create permanent wall-hangings for a long corridor.
- Puppet making, when a retired teacher worked with children to make a full set of suitably dressed nativity stick puppets with papier mâché heads.
- Joint abstract paintings on canvas that were hung in the library.

In order to sustain interest and involvement, you could plan to have a large-scale school art exhibition towards the end of the year, where the children can choose their own best pieces made during the year, or have the opportunity to make something new based on their previous experiences. They could help to plan the exhibition, including making suggestions about how the artwork could be displayed, writing invitations and organising refreshments. The exhibition could include certificates or prizes for different categories with the whole school having the chance to vote.

Partnerships with parents

Forging positive relationships with parents is important in so many ways but can also be a great boost to creativity. See Box 5.2 for some suggestions. Valuing, in a tangible way, what parents may have to offer can have long-lasting and important effects for school, parent and child alike. Not only will you be capitalising upon the skills and talents the parents bring, but they will also be learning about how their child learns, and the skills which they possess that may not be apparent at home. When parents have this kind of knowledge there is a greater chance that children will extend their learning beyond the classroom so that they have started on the ladder of lifelong learning. As there are often time restraints in school, having knowledgeable and willing parents on your side will mean that children are more likely to develop their own creative projects at home, using the skills, knowledge and understanding that they have been taught in school. In our view, a key test of how motivating activities at school are is whether children choose to do them at home.

Box 5.2   Ideas for parental input

- Invent maths games.
- Make story boxes, story sacks or role-play sacks.
- Help to create dual-language texts for use in the classroom.
- Create book-based board games.

- Help children to run the library.
- Talk to children, or staff, about particular areas of expertise, interesting experiences or so that they can share specialist knowledge.
- Tell stories, especially stories from different cultures.
- Come in at lunchtimes to share playground games or 'wet play' activities.
- Run after-school clubs in which the parent has a particular interest, e.g. sports clubs, scrap-booking, musical tuition, local history, computers, etc.
- Provide regular support in art sessions.
- Help with preparation for special events such as school parties or performances.

Partnerships with local organisations

Enlisting the help of local organisations can not only develop good community links, but also allows children to develop interests beyond those normally available to them, so that they can connect with the world around them, reflect upon their own experiences and be challenged to engage creatively with new opportunities.

The local council

As we write, environmental issues continue to grow in importance. Children often have a natural interest in the environment. Local councils are also heavily involved in environmental issues. As part of Agenda 21, the international community's response to global environmental issues, every council must state how it is going to tackle such issues locally. Children can become actively involved in developing a school response that supports what the local council have pledged to do. Local transport issues could be another area that may be of interest, or the development of land for housing.

Emergency services

The local fire, police, ambulance or coastguard services are usually happy to be involved with school projects that raise pupils' awareness of safety and community issues. For example, one local police community officer organised a poster competition for children to tackle the problem of graffiti in their area, while another school developed close links with a nearby fire station. As part of this, the school discovered that the site had not always been used for this purpose and unexpectedly began on a search to find out how the land had been used in the past.

Local history groups

As sources of much local knowledge that may not be found in other ways, members of local history groups can be approached to work with you on your own local history projects. The children can devise their own sets of questions as a basis for the work, which will set them off on the next part of their project. Using such local experts can be invaluable in developing children's interests as well as their interpersonal and questioning skills.

Partnerships with local businesses

Banks

Some high-street banks offer schools the chance to have their own operational branch within the school, which is run by the children with adult help and for which training is provided. As well as helping children to develop their own economic understanding, this is a creative way for children to work with adults other than their usual teacher while enhancing their self-esteem and being helped to develop mathematical and social skills.

Travel agents

Making your role-play area into a travel agent's offers the possibility for children to visit a local agent, or to invite a representative to come to school. The children can then suggest what should be included in the area, on the advice of their local expert. For older pupils, this could form the basis for a project linking geography and maths as well as aspects of literacy.

Manufacturing industries

While health and safety regulations make it increasingly difficult for children to visit factories or workplaces, local firms' websites can be explored, and staff can be invited to come and talk in school. This could form the basis for children developing their own manufacturing 'company', where a product of their choice is selected, designed, tested and refined. This could range from food products such as biscuits, cakes, drinks or sandwiches, to items like greetings cards, bags or pottery creations. You may even be able to sell them!

6 The Mantle of the Expert

Drama and role play have a unique contribution to make to creativity. The technique called Mantle of the Expert, developed in the 1980s by Dorothy Heathcote, originally a drama teacher and later of the University of Newcastle, uses an approach to learning sometimes referred to as a 'community of enquiry', where children take on the responsibility for running an enterprise in a fictional world, through which knowledge, skills and understanding are developed. The approach uses drama as a basis for a pedagogy rooted in the belief that children will learn best when their motivation and engagement are fostered, and treats the children as though they were experts in a particular field. They metaphorically put on the 'mantle' of an expert within a dramatic context that provides the basis for their learning. As well as fulfilling the requirements of the National Curriculum, using the Mantle approach offers not only a wealth of creative possibilities, but also a particular opportunity for children to develop both imagination and empathy, and to take account of many of the constituents of the social and emotional aspects of learning (SEAL).

When a class is engaged in this type of learning, both teacher and pupils work in role within an imaginary community. The children are treated as experts in some area. This may be a commercial enterprise, where their 'company' offers a service such as looking after pets when owners go on holiday, or planning special events. They may be expert archaeologists, detectives or problem solvers. Or perhaps they are conservationists working in a particular field such as caring for an endangered species, or looking after a threatened woodland or wetland area. They may be a rescue organisation or a group of conservators. The fact that they are not actually experts in these areas at the start does not matter. Being treated as though they were is enough; the skills they will be using and developing alongside the possibilities for creative engagement are more important to their real learning than the acquisition of facts.

Being in role does not mean dressing up or putting on a funny voice; you work seriously with the children as though they really were experts in the area chosen for the frame within which you are working. You are all 'in' the story.

The teacher acts very much as facilitator, with much of the decision making about the direction that the learning will take being handed over to the children. Because of this, they feel an increased sense of ownership; this type of learning is not done *to* them but *by* them. They have a vested interest and therefore a serious involvement, which results in the possibility of higher levels of achievement. This does not mean that no prior planning is involved – far from it; considerable thought must be given to planning the context for the learning and considering the possible routes that may follow, together with the outcomes that may be generated.

While you will have a good idea of the ways in which the work will develop, and still retain overall control in order to guide things your way, remember that the children may steer the project into a different direction. You need to be prepared for this by thinking through the possibilities that your initial stimulus, and following structures and intervention, may have. When children devise a creative solution to a problem, be prepared to go with it even if you foresee pitfalls. Far better for the children to discover these for themselves, and learn from the situation. This may mean that you revisit your planning once the mantle is under way, deleting or adding activities and trajectories retrospectively. If your initial planning has notes and annotations added, it shows that it is a real working document and that you are not being hidebound by your own ideas; rather, you are adapting to suit the creativity of your class.

The approach has also received some official approval. At a Mantle of the Expert conference in July 2006, Mick Waters, from the QCA, spoke in favour. There are also examples of OfSTED praising schools that have included this approach, such as two East Anglian schools that work in this way, despite the fact that 'lessons' often do not have a specific outcome and do not start with a stated learning objective. Learning objectives can be very limiting, and can stifle creativity.

There is no rigid timetabling once the approach is fully up and running, so there are fewer constraints upon developing the learning. However, it is possible to have 'mini-mantles' within the confines of normal timetabling, and this could be a starting point for newcomers to this way of working.

Where do I start?

The old key

Doorways can lead anywhere, and that is the conceit behind this idea that you could use as a first foray into using Mantle of the Expert. This may last for one long session, or could run to two or three, depending on the direction in which the learning goes. It may help to seat the children in a circle.

- Explain briefly to the class that today you are going to be trying out a new way of working in which you will be taking on the role of someone else. Instead of being yourself, for this session you will be a police constable, a museum curator, or someone from the lost property department (you choose).
- Once in role, begin by showing them a key that has been found. This could be a real key, particularly if you are working with very young children, or you could simply draw a key on paper. As Mantle demands the use of the imagination, costly props or resources are rarely needed. Tell them that you have heard they are experts in solving problems (maybe they are detectives?), and you would like them to help you to find out what the key opens, and maybe who it belongs to. You could add that it was found hidden, so you are rather suspicious. It doesn't seem like an ordinary key. They will be hooked and will most definitely want to help!
- Ask if anyone has any ideas about what the key might fit. In your role, you could write these suggestions in your official notebook. You may want to follow up some of the

suggestions with questions such as the ones below to make the children think more deeply and give reasons for their ideas:
- 'So, what makes you think that, then?'
- 'Can you tell me why you think that?'
- 'Have you had any experience of that kind of thing?'
- 'Do you have any evidence for suggesting that?'

- Ultimately you want the key to open some sort of doorway or gateway, or perhaps even a portal, so follow through the suggestions that are going in that direction. You could say, 'I think you may be right – I seem to remember someone reporting they had lost a key like that', or 'Now that you mention it, it does look a bit like a key that would open a church/old house/bank/prison/blocked tunnel/secret garden'.

- Step out of role now briefly, to tell the children that you are going to move the story on. You will now be in front of the doorway, with the key in your hand. Ask the children to stand. Now you are back in role. 'Have you got the key? I think we should try it in the lock. I tried knocking, but there was no reply.' Mime putting the key in the lock, along with the children. As you do so, say, 'It seems to fit. It feels a bit stiff, though. Aah – yes. It definitely fits. It's very hard but it is turning. It's worked!'

- It is crucial at this point that no one goes through the doorway, so say, 'Wait! We don't know what's behind this door. I think we'd better stop and think before we go through.'

- At this point, you generate a discussion about what might be behind the door. What suggestions do the children have? Could it be dangerous? Should you let someone know? Might you need some special equipment before you go through? What if someone is there? It is probably not sensible just to go straight in. What's needed is a plan. Ask the children to make one, in any form, to outline what should be done. The plans will vary, of course, depending on what kind of doorway is being investigated. Some may decide to have a hinged flap in the form of a doorway that opens to reveal what might be inside.

- As the children are working, circulate around the room asking questions about their plans and if necessary prompting ideas by asking, 'What if . . .?' or 'Have you thought of . . .?' questions (remember you are still in role). It will be particularly important that they know how they are going to come back out again. Do they have plans for what to do if something goes wrong?

- The next step is to put the plans into action. The children use their keys to unlock and now open the door, to find out what really is inside. You may do this collectively, or in small groups. Use prompts if necessary, such as:
  - 'Can you see? Do you need to use a torch, or find a light switch?'
  - 'What can you see/hear/smell?'
  - 'Is anyone there?'
  - 'What is actually behind the door? Is it what you expected, or something else?'
  - 'Are there any clues about who lives or works there?'
  - 'Are you going to take any photographs or make any notes about what you can see or have found?'
  - 'Will you use your mobile phone to contact anyone before you leave?'

  When you sense that enough time has been spent on this, say, 'I think it's time we left. Make sure you lock the door again when you go.'

- Once safely back outside, you can have a discussion about what happened on the other side of the door, before asking the children to write their expert's report on the investigation.

The mystery box

This mini-mantle once again uses the children's curiosity to hook them in.

- You are in role as someone who has just moved house. You bought a second-hand chest of drawers inside which you have found a box. For this scenario, you will have put together a real box, inside which are a number of objects that may or may not have some link. Perhaps there's a part of a letter, a train ticket, a receipt, an old pair of glasses, a key ring with a few keys on, some foreign coins, a special pebble, a photograph, or any other interesting items.
- You ask the children for their suggestions about what kind of person the box might have belonged to. Start by taking suggestions from the class before groups of children investigate each of the items more closely. Ask them to make notes about their ideas, but tell them that they should be prepared to explain their thinking. One way of doing this is to use Post-it notes that are stuck on to a working wall under labels for each item. This way everyone can see the picture being produced of a possible owner.
- Next, draw the class together again to sum up their thinking. Does this point towards an owner? Or are there several possibilities? When hearing the views of others, does anyone want to change their mind?
- Ask the children to draw a picture of what they think the owner looks like, with speech bubbles telling us about some of the items in the box, in the owner's words. Alternatively, the children could write in role as the owner, either explaining some or all of the items, or relating the story of the significance of just one item.

Longer units

Mantles that are designed to last over several sessions, or weeks, obviously require more planning. Start by looking at the long-term plan for your year, based on National Curriculum requirements, to see which elements could be linked together. For example, here are the areas that Liz, a Year 3 teacher, planned to include in a mantle, where her class was to be in role as a travel company that specialised in planning and organising individually tailored holidays for clients:

- **History** – ancient Greeks
- **Literacy** – myths and legends, information texts, speaking and listening, drama, writing: in role, lists, letters, logos, instructions, reports, recounts, information, captions, adverts, posters
- **Mathematics** – Money, Time, Data Handling
- **Geography** – Weather round the World; Maps
- **Art** – drawing, painting, pottery
- **Design and technology** – planning an exhibition and artefacts for Greek Experience Day
- **ICT** – internet searching, PowerPoint, desktop publishing
- **Physical education** – athletics linked to the Olympic Games
- **Personal, social, health and economic education** – disability issues.

It is important, when choosing the enterprise that determines the role or expertise to be the focus, that it is something that the children will find interesting. Animals are always popular, so working in role as zookeepers, wildlife park staff or conservationists works well. You then decide on the 'hook' to initiate the work. This could be a letter, phone call or e-mail that has been received by the company or organisation the children represent, asking for their help or inviting them to do some work for a client. Or you could initiate the enterprise by acting in role and speaking directly to the class as though you were consulting them in their expert capacity.

Selecting your own role in the enterprise is important. If you remain as the teacher, the mantle will not feel as 'real', and the children will expect you to fulfil your usual role. When you assume a different role, you can legitimately plead ignorance, which leads to greater independence on the part of the children, and determines the need for them to think for themselves to a greater degree, necessitating more use of problem-solving strategies and creative solutions. So, you could be a representative of the commissioning company, or the office manager for example, so that you do retain some degree of control allowing you to tie things together, or change the direction of the activities if it becomes necessary. You are effectively the gatekeeper.

It is worth bearing in mind that, as with any fictional work, a history is assumed. Nothing starts at the very beginning, so when a new mantle is begun, there is already a background. This can be used to great advantage, as you will see in the example below. Incidentally, have no fears that the children will not enter into the fiction; you will be surprised at how easily and eagerly they suspend disbelief. This is, after all, an extension of their normal play world.

Joanne, a Year 4 teacher, had introduced her class to the idea of working in role within a community of enquiry using the mystery box idea, and felt ready to try a longer unit. She chose a scientific basis, linking plant growth and habitats through using the school environment and local community. She had a specific literacy focus of writing development. She was also keen to develop the children's self-esteem and empathy. Here is what she did, over several weeks, taking the children on a learning journey.

A garden for the blind

- Joanne told the class that they (including herself), as garden design experts Gardens R Us, had received a letter. She showed them the actual letter (which of course she had written; see Box 6.1), and then a large version on the interactive whiteboard.

Box 6.1 Teacher's letter initiating a garden for blind people

Planners Incorporated

Dear Gardens R Us

We have heard a lot about your interesting garden design projects and would like you to provide some ideas for a special garden that we have been asked to construct for one of our clients.

This is to be a garden for partially sighted and blind people, so we know that this will present you with quite a challenge. However, we know from your previous work that you will no doubt come up with some exciting ideas that will work well. We are sure you will take health and safety issues into account when drawing up your suggested designs.

We have no restrictions on the shape or size of the garden, but we do know that this is a completely empty area, with no existing trees or buildings to be taken into consideration. All we need at this stage are your suggestions for the types of plants that might be included, together with some layout designs that will be workable for partially sighted and blind people.

We look forward to seeing your designs.

Yours sincerely

- Joanne drew particular attention to the fact that the client already knew about their work:

  Joanne: I wonder which of our designs they know about? Which ones can you remember?

  Child A: The Disney one we did in Paris.

  Child B: That one like in Jamaica, where my dad comes from.

  Child C: And the football one for the World Cup.

  The children had immediately begun to 'remember' previous commissions, which of course had happened not in reality, but in the world of the Mantle. After several other suggestions, Joanne guided the conversation in another direction: 'I think it might be helpful to plot this. Does anyone know if we have a long piece of paper?' Someone spotted a roll of wallpaper Joanne had already left lying on a table; the furniture was moved back, the paper rolled out on the floor with everyone kneeling around its length. 'Now then, do you remember when we did that Disney garden?' 'About six years ago.' From this, Joanne began to build a timeline on the paper, showing when the different gardens were created, adding extra information about them as it was volunteered. When the children could see the process, she handed over to them to continue the timeline, adding their own garden projects to it. Thus, a company history was created.

- Next, Joanne asked which of the children had been with the company since it started ('I can't quite remember – can you?'). Individual autobiographies began to emerge, including one boy who used to be a policeman but wasn't enjoying his job, so decided to change careers. His role in the company was to work on-site, digging and planting. A girl and two boys emerged as the original creators of the company, ten years previously. They had met at gardening college, where the girl worked in the cafeteria and one of the boys was a taxi driver in his spare time, to earn extra money. They were now the general managers, seeking out new clients and organising the work of others. Joanne volunteered her own story and asked the children to write their auto-biographies for the company file.

- They now returned to the original letter, and the request for a design for a garden for the blind. 'This sounds difficult', said Joanne. 'I wonder what special things we'll have to consider?' This sparked a conversation about the obvious problems, and small groups of children set about making designs on paper. These formed the basis for much further discussion, with Joanne in role posing difficult questions about practicalities. Children compared their designs and refined them.
- This stage also involved research into plants, and a visit to the local garden allotment society was arranged to find out more information.
- Joanne was still not satisfied that the suggestions would meet the client's brief, and drew the children back to the part of the letter where health and safety aspects were mentioned. 'How could we find out what it is actually like for a blind person to walk around a garden?' she asked, and someone suggested walking round the school grounds with closed eyes. They did this, realising difficulties they had not anticipated, such as changes in level, how to find your way round the garden, and the problems of spiky plants and stinging nettles. These problems had to be solved, and children devised their own ways of overcoming them. For instance, they noticed that they could tell when they were walking on grass or bark chippings, and realised this could be used to advantage in defining different areas of the garden. The notion of a rope handrail to act as a guide was suggested, and eliminating dangerous plants was seen as important, as was including scented plants and plants with different textures to the leaves. So then it was back to the drawing board, to adapt their original plans.

It is important to have a clear endpoint to a mantle; in this case, the children wrote letters to the client, explaining what they had done and inviting them to see a display of their finished annotated designs. The teaching assistant took the role of the client, and discussed the designs and their execution with the young designers.

While the work was going on, the children were aware that they were 'in a story', and Joanne knew that at any time she could step outside the world of the mantle into the world of the classroom, in order to re-establish her role as teacher. This can be done if, for example, within the story it becomes necessary to write a letter and instruction is needed in how to do this correctly. The teacher simply stops the story to go back to the world of the classroom where the children can learn the skill they need. Once this has been achieved, they step back into the story, where time has effectively stood still, waiting for them.

The Iron Man

Steve carried out a much longer-term mantle with a Year 4 class, based on Ted Hughes' classic book *The Iron Man*. Here the class became a fictional company called Film Kit, whose expertise was in designing and making props for film companies. Steve's chosen role was as on-site representative of a film company that had commissioned Film Kit to make models of the Iron Man for a forthcoming live-action animation. Steve started the Mantle in the same way as Joanne had done, with a letter from the film company that led into creating a company history and a timeline. From this point, each child decided upon their role within Film Kit and wrote their own job descriptions. They were then asked to work out what skills and knowledge they would need in order to fulfil the commission, and Steve used these as a basis for future work. Of course, he had already planned what most of this work would be, knowing that the children would need to know the story, which he would read to them. They would also need to know how to create stop-frame animations, which he planned to teach in the world of the classroom.

While the children were engaged with their mantle work, Steve made use of the 'overheard conversation' to extend the drama outside the working space. Using an imaginary telephone, he would both make and receive phone calls from his boss, Linda, who had to be kept informed on progress. This device allowed Steve to call a halt or move things on when he could see that this was necessary. For example, the children would overhear him saying, 'Yes, all right, Linda, I'll tell them. But they've already done quite a lot of work on that. What? Are you saying you want them to change it all? Well, they won't be happy, but I'll do my best.' Steve could then relate the full conversation to the class, saying that Linda needed, for example, a list of equipment, or a scripted dialogue of the planned scene.

Steve knew that there was already an animated version of the story, but that it was very different from the book, so he had also planned to show that to the children, while they were in role, in order to compare the two versions and to see how animators worked. He also found a website (www.filmstsreet.co.uk) that gave children the opportunity to learn more about animations, which several followed up at home. The children were then able to create storyboards of the scene they had chosen to animate.

Children designed and made their Iron Man models from card, boxes and foil, but only after they had made some stop-frame animations using a computer program and simple digital video recorder. This helped them to realise that the size of the model was important if it were to fit the frame. Backgrounds also had to be designed for the filming of a chosen scene, and dialogue scripted and rehearsed.

Steve planned a large number of drama activities (see Box 6.2 for examples) that took place out of the mantle story, but supported it, in order to give them a full understanding of the characters. This involved the children acting in a variety of roles.

Box 6.2   Iron Man drama activities

Use of drama conventions based on *The Iron Man* by Ted Hughes

Chapter 2

- Freeze-frame the first farmer's reactions to his tractor being half-eaten by the Iron Man.
- Dialogue between two farmers who have both had machinery eaten. After rehearsal, the rest of the group overhear their conversation.
- Dialogue between small groups of farmers when they plan the digging of the pit to trap the Iron Man. After rehearsal, the rest of the group overhear their conversation.

Chapter 3

- p. 28. Recreate scene of family picnic on the hill that covers the Iron Man. Perform as if running a video. The group can stop it at any moment to ask characters questions.

- p. 31. Farmers see and describe the Iron Man for the first time – dialogue as overheard conversation. They creep up; take photos. Can show photos to third member who was not present at the time.
- p. 32. Hogarth apologises to the Iron Man and offers solutions – overheard monologue. One person in role as the Iron Man, but unable to reply, though can use body/facial reactions.
- p. 32. Follow-up: Hogarth in the Hot Seat.
- p. 33. Freeze-frame villagers' reactions to seeing the Iron Man come down the street.
- Freeze-frame the Iron Man happy in the scrapyard.
- Role on the wall – Iron Man.
- Hot-seat the Iron Man.

Chapter 4

- pp. 37–39. In role as astronomers discussing the changing 'star'.
- Written report read out to second group (perhaps politicians) on findings following observations.
- pp. 40–45. Use as a basis for debate: the threat posed by the dragon – what are we going to do? What are the problems? Formal discussion following astronomers' reports.
- Dragon as role on the wall.
- Dragon in Conscience Alley.

The mantle ended when Laura, a colleague from another school, visited Film Kit in role as Steve's boss, Linda. She talked with the children, saw their models and their animations, congratulated them on their achievements and wished them luck in any future projects.

For more information and news of current events, visit www.mantleoftheexpert.com.

Role play in other contexts

Mantle of the Expert is not, of course, the only way to use role play to enhance the curriculum. Giving children virtual first-hand experience deepens their understanding and can lead to their having new perspectives and ideas. Here are some examples.

Jungle adventure

Stacey, an early years practitioner, took over both the school hall and part of the school grounds to create a jungle adventure day for her class. They had previously been reading books such as Michael Rosen's *We're going on a bear hunt* and Tony Mitton's *Rumble in the jungle*. They had also used bears as a focus for activities. The evening before the jungle day, Stacey and her teaching assistant had set up the hall to look like a jungle:

- Camouflage netting was hung over the large climbing frame.
- Fabrics and sacking were draped over PE equipment.
- As many potted plants as possible were placed around the scene.
- Dens containing cuddly toy bears and other creatures, cooking pots and pans, and writing materials were improvised.
- Jungle sound effects were set up to play in the background.
- The outside area had illustrated notices put up warning 'Danger! Beware of the wild animals!' 'Bears ahead', and 'Thick mud. Watch out!'
- Toy animals and large plastic insects were placed among the trees and bushes.

The children came to school dressed in suitable expedition clothes, and of course brought an explorer's packed lunch. They had already made cardboard binoculars and cameras ready for the event. They were issued with passports for the day, and lined up at the check-in desk to board the plane to the jungle.

Stacey was particularly fortunate in having a volunteer grandad who ran a lunchtime simulated flying club for older pupils, using a computer program. He used this program, run through the interactive whiteboard, to give the children a real sense of being on board a plane. Stacey helped this by arranging the chairs in airline style. An alternative to this luxury would be to use the tilt and move facility on Google Earth, which gives a similar flying sensation.

Once at their destination, the group left the 'plane' to walk to the jungle; one half of the class visiting each location to explore, looking through their binoculars, taking photographs of what they found, making notes in their explorer's notebooks and writing postcards home.

The Queen's coronation

Angela, a Year 1 teacher, planned a unit of work based around celebrations, one of which had a historical focus, looking at how the Queen's coronation was celebrated in 1953. Angela used role play in two ways: by recreating the actual coronation with a child representing the Queen, appropriately dressed and seated on a specially decorated chair, while other children took on the roles of those involved in the ceremony or were part of the congregation. Music from the coronation service was played to accompany the re-creation.

The second use of role play involved having a street party on the playground, for which the children had made the food themselves (with adult helpers). They designed and made party hats, bunting and Union Jack flags, and sang songs of the period, including the national anthem. Following this, they were able to draw and write about their experiences.

The Fire of London

In a Year 2 class, Sarah used the Fire of London as a basis for role play, with the diary of Samuel Pepys providing the stimulus. Once they had been told the story, the children made freeze-frames of the original outbreak of the fire in the Pudding Lane baker's shop, the reactions of townsfolk as the fire spread, and Pepys watching the fire from a safe distance. Sarah then used thought-tracking, asking children what they were thinking as they experienced the fire.

Pairs of children later improvised conversations when, in role, they revisited the charred remains of their homes. They then enjoyed creating their own diary entries on paper that they had stained with teabags and singed at the edges, which made an effective display.

Theseus and the Minotaur

Victoria in Year 3 was studying the ancient Greeks and used role play to help her pupils gain a greater understanding of the Greek myths. Having read the story of Theseus and the Minotaur to the class, Victoria led them into the labyrinth, in role as Theseus, acting out the story aloud as she went. They struggled to see in the darkness, using their senses to try to find their way through. Finally they encountered the Minotaur, and the inevitable fight ensued. Victorious, they found Ariadne's thread, which led them back out to the welcoming and grateful crowd.

Victoria followed this up with freeze-framing, thought tracking, and role on the wall, where the children stuck Post-it notes on to an outline of Theseus, saying what he had seen, heard, smelt and felt before, during and after he entered the labyrinth. Box 6.3 shows some extracts from the writing that resulted.

Box 6.3 Theseus and the Minotaur: examples of children's writing

He took the ball of string off Ariadne and entered the very very dark slimy labyrinth. He had many twists and turns. He felt like bones were crunching each time he took a step.

By Tatum, aged 7

Suddenly I saw two huge red eyes staring at me so I got out my sword and finally I started to fight him. I poked my sword and finally I got him in the heart. He fell to the ground. I was glad but I forgot all about the ball of string I needed to get back! So I had to get on my hands and knees and crawl on the slimy floor to find it.

By Brioni, aged 8

When I walked in I heard something echoing in the distance a long way away. It was scary when I went in. It was so dark that I nearly fell over. The floor was sticky and horrible like jelly. I can hear that noise going on. I can hear it getting closer and closer. I can kill him, I bet I can. The floor is moving, the walls are jumping. Oh no! I dropped my string!

By Emily, aged 8

I was entering the maze and holding the ball of string tightly. The walls were as sticky as a lolly licked one million times. I did not like it at all. I wish it was light, I can't see a thing. Is that a puff of breath I can see? Maybe the Minotaur will be round the next corner! I anxiously turned the next corner and bumped into something big and furry. It had long dainty claws. It tore at my clothes and scratched my shoulder.

By Lydia, aged 8

An Indian wedding

As part of her religious education programme, Cath, a Year 4 teacher, planned a re-creation of a Hindu wedding ceremony. A bride and groom were chosen, as were other family members, the officiating priest and the guests. A parent had provided a selection of traditional Indian clothing for the main characters to look the part, the room was set up to represent the setting, and traditional food was prepared. The ceremony duly took place, with photographs being taken of each section.

This was a particularly important experience for Cath's class, as they live in a rural area where faiths other than Christianity are rarely represented in the community. This role play gave them a chance to discover more about Hinduism, in a meaningful way.

A Kenyan village

Andrew's Year 6 class were studying Kenya as a country in the developing world. They had been looking at similarities and differences between life in a Kenyan village and in their own town, as well as finding out about life in Kenyan cities. Andrew decided to use a debate in role to help the children understand more about why young people move from a rural life to urban locations, by using the notion of push–pull factors.

Andrew played the part of someone trying to decide whether to stay living in the village, or to move to the city. He divided the class into two groups, one acting as villagers trying to persuade him to stay, while the other was in role as city-dwellers, providing the opposing argument. The children needed to bring all their knowledge to bear in trying to win Andrew over. They had to listen to the opposing views and counter them with an appropriate argument. If the debate flagged a little, Andrew intervened with a suitable prompt such as 'But what if I miss my friends?' or 'I'm sure life will be much more interesting in the city.'

Role-play areas

The role-play area has traditionally been confined to the early years classroom, where it is used most imaginatively. But there is no reason why role-play areas cannot be extended across the primary school. Some possibilities are:

- a vet's practice when studying animals;
- a French café, to support the teaching of the language;
- a hospital department or doctor's surgery linked to learning about the human body;
- a storytelling corner for children to read or retell stories to their friends;
- a Victorian school, showing the differences between then and now;
- a kitchen, to link with healthy schools work;
- a Greek theatre, with masks, to support work on the ancient Greeks;
- a garden shed, when studying plants and growth;
- a laboratory for testing materials;
- a bank when teaching money.

7 Thinking skills

The teaching of thinking skills, when done well, helps children to engage in a greater range of thought than they otherwise would. This range reflects divergent thinking, something that has been linked with creativity. An emphasis on thinking skills is often a reaction against transmission teaching, which focuses on the learning of information, often in an uncritical way. We are not arguing that the accumulation of information, some of which requires memorisation, is completely without value. In fact, in order to be creative it is necessary to acquire knowledge and understanding in relation to the field of enquiry. But we are arguing that teaching children to think more clearly, and to have an open mind, is a necessary part of effective teaching and is something that is likely to enhance creativity. Formal recognition of the importance of thinking skills comes from the Five Key Thinking Skills that are included as a guiding principle in the National Curriculum, and should be part of the planning and teaching process.

There are various ways into teaching thinking skills. We begin this chapter with an introductory activity that you might try. We then cover one of the most popular approaches, Edward de Bono's Thinking Hats. Encouraging children to hypothesise and speculate about the very biggest questions such as: Is there a God? How far is it to the edge of the universe? Is time travel possible? takes us into the realm of philosophy for children. Finally, the chapter has a reminder about the value of visual strategies to encourage thinking.

Thinking about thinking

A good introductory activity is to encourage children to think about thinking! Here are some questions to try:

- What is thinking?
- What part of our body do we think with?
- Do we all think in the same way?
- Do we think in words, pictures or something else?
- Do children think in the same ways as adults?
- Do animals think?
- Do we think when we are asleep?

Some responses from a Year 4 class were:

> 'We think with our brain, but not all of it.'

> 'We don't all think the same. Some of us think deeply and others think on the outside.'

> 'We don't think in the same way because we are all different.'

> 'Children don't think the same as adults because children might be thinking about their future and adults might be thinking about their children.'

> 'Animals probably do think because they would have to think about what they're going to eat and drink, and how they are going to defend themselves against other animals.'

> 'We do think when we're asleep, because when you dream, that's basically the same as thinking, but when you dream you probably dream about things you would not think about. When you think, you can control your thoughts, but when you dream, you can't.'

One of the best-known writers on thinking is Edward de Bono. His work on thinking was originally geared towards adults in the business world, rather than children in the classroom, but has since been developed and used effectively in schools. One of his techniques has been particularly popular.

De Bono's thinking hats

The basic premise of using de Bono's six 'thinking hats' is that there is more than one way to think about things. Each thinking hat represents a different way of considering a proposition, statement or situation.

The white hat	deals only with the facts
The black hat	considers potential difficulties
The yellow hat	focuses on positive elements
The red hat	allows for feelings about the idea to be put forward
The green hat	offers solutions that may be idealistic or unusual
The blue hat	takes account of all the other hats in order to arrive at a solution

Each of the first five hats has equal weight, so that the person wearing the red hat, representing feelings, who says, 'I don't know why, but this just doesn't feel right', has as much validity as the person in the white hat, representing facts, who can present data supporting the suggestion. The increased awareness we now have of the importance of the social and emotional aspects of learning acknowledges that we are less likely to learn when we are not feeling positive, so the red hat acts as a tangible reminder that people's feelings about a situation should be taken into account and not dismissed simply because they cannot be backed up by attributable data. It is not necessary in this activity to articulate a reason for the feeling.

When you first introduce the idea of thinking hats to your class, do it gradually, with one or two hats at a time, so that the children can assimilate how each hat works. Some teachers use pictures of hats, but having actual hats that you and the children can wear works even better. These can be bought cheaply, or even made from paper. The hats do not have to be of uniform design.

Introducing the white hat

Learning how to focus on facts helps to develop an understanding of how to take an objective view.

- Tell the children that when we wear the white hat, we are only thinking about facts and information. Display a large image of the hat, or wear it.
- A historic context can work well. Show a portrait of a historic character, perhaps Henry VIII or Tutankhamun, and ask, 'What facts do we know about this person?' Once the list is complete, check with the class that everything is actually a fact or piece of information that could, as far as possible, be supported with evidence of one kind or another.
- In a second session, while wearing or showing the hat, display an image on the interactive whiteboard of a person in a setting. This could be anything from a child on the beach to a Victorian portrait. Ask the same question: 'What do we know about this?' once again scribing responses, fielding off answers that are not supportable facts, and checking the final list. If the image were a child on the beach, your list might include the following:
  - It's a photograph.
  - It's a boy.
  - He is wearing blue Wellingtons, blue shorts and a red T-shirt.
  - There is no one else near him.
  - He is on sand and next to some water.
  - There is a green bucket near his right hand.
  - He has a red spade in his left hand.
  - He is bending over and the spade is stuck into a shallow hole in the sand.
  - It is not raining.
  - It is daytime.
- Next, give pairs or small groups of children a sheet with an image of a different person in a different setting. Together they write or draw their own list of white hat facts about the image. To reinforce the notion of the white hat, this could be drawn on the sheet, or simple white paper hats could be worn by at least one of the children in each group.

Building up the whole picture

There is no particular order in which to introduce the hats, but Melanie asked her Year 3 class to consider the possibility of having boys and girls in separate classes as the context for understanding how the yellow, black and red hats worked.

Before using the hats, Melanie asked the class to vote yes or no to the suggestion, and noted the outcome. Then, after explaining what each hat represented, she gave pairs of children a recording sheet with a simple three-column grid, each with a colour picture of one of the hats at the top. Together the children discussed and noted the potential yellow hat positive and black hat negative issues posed by the suggestion, as well as their own feelings about it. This led to a whole-class discussion and a second vote, before which Melanie asked the children to consider everyone's points. As the totals for and against the suggestion had changed, Melanie asked whether anyone could explain why they had altered their opinions, receiving answers such as

> 'I hadn't thought about all the other things people said.'

> 'I thought it would be good to have all the girls together, because the boys annoy me, but now I think it might be boring.'

> 'When I looked at what I'd written, I had more things for the black hat than the yellow one, so I had to change my mind.'

When the children are familiar with the functions of each of the hats, they can be used to facilitate thinking in many ways. Ruth, in Year 4, used them to help her class to use paragraphing in non-fiction writing. Her class were writing reports on the effects of global warming and used the hats to help, so the white hat presented facts objectively, the black hat explained the problems, and so on. Once each aspect had been planned in note form, the children used these to write one paragraph for each hat, ending with the blue hat, where they drew all the elements together to present their own overall conclusion. Figures 7.1–7.3 show examples of their work.

In Ruth's example, the children were working independently, with the thinking hats linked to individual children, but the thinking hats approach can also act as an aid to group work. For example, the class could be divided into five groups, each group being given one hat to wear to consider a particular idea or problem.

If the problem is a real one, within the children's experience, its relevance will make the exercise more worthwhile. It is likely that there will be something to do with the school that can be used for this. It may be to do with movement around the school, difficulties with lunch arrangements, or perhaps use of shared resources such as computers or the hall. When each group has reported back, the whole class wears the blue hat to arrive at a joint conclusion, or the groups can have a class debate, with each hat representing a different perspective. Alternatively, each member of a group could wear a different hat, presenting the appropriate view. The child with the blue hat acts as listener and scribe, reporting back to the whole class. What this process does is to help the children to realise that they can approach problems and decision making in a constructive way, and aids the social and emotional aspects of learning, for example by developing empathy as the different viewpoints have to be considered. Sarah used the six hats to tackle the problems caused by some children playing football at lunchtimes. Table 7.1 shows some of the children's responses.

Philosophy for children

Robert Fisher has long advocated the use of philosophy in schools. His specially written stories are designed to provoke responses that can lead to philosophical discussion and the development of thinking skills. Having heard or read the story, children are invited to think about questions arising from it that are philosophical in nature – questions that

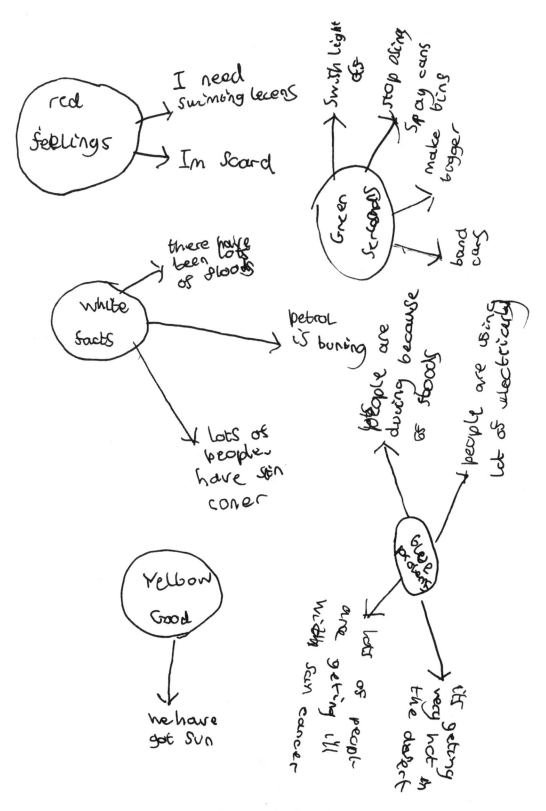

Figure 7.1 Using 'thinking hats' to note ideas about global warming

Global warnings

Global Warning is damaging our world. It is Very dangerous and is causing lots of floods.

Global warning is bad and it has to stop. There are lots of problems like people getting ill and dying.

However there is one good thing and that is we are getting lots of good weather.

I feel terrible about global warning because I am not helping much and if something bad happens to this world I would feel scared and sad.

There are plenty of solutions. We could reycicle, walk alot and don't drive and turn off lights also have our own global warning T.V programme.

We could phone up T.V people and tell them to tell people to stop global warning.

Figure 7.2 A child's paragraphs about global warming, following the use of 'thinking hats'

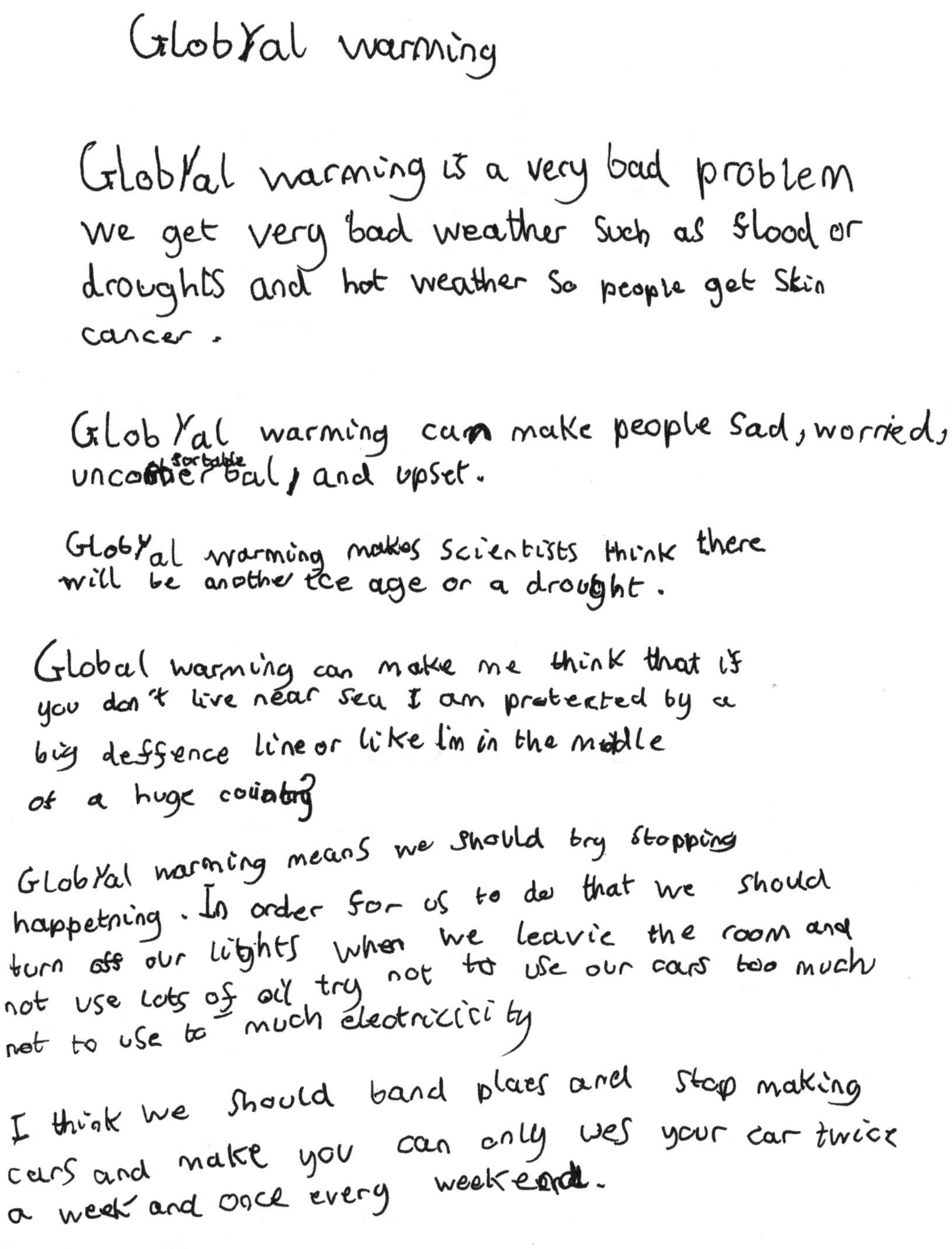

Globlyal warming

Globlyal warming is a very bad problem
we get very bad weather such as flood or
droughts and hot weather so people get skin
cancer.

Globlyal warming cum make people sad, worried,
uncomfortable, and upset.

Globlyal warming makes scientists think there
will be another ice age or a drought.

Global warming can make me think that if
you don't live near sea I am protected by a
big deffence line or like I'm in the middle
of a huge country

Globlyal warming means we should try stopping
happetning. In order for us to do that we should
turn off our lights when we leavie the room and
not use lots of oil try not to use our cars too much
not to use to much electriciciity

I think we should band plaes and stop making
cars and make you can only wes your car twice
a week and once every weekend.

Figure 7.3 A child's paragraphs about global warming, following the use of 'thinking hats': second example

Table 7.1 *Thinking about football*

White hat	Black hat	Yellow hat	Red hat	Green hat
• Mostly boys play • Different year groups don't mix together • It gives you exercise • People get muddy sometimes	• You might get injured • Sometimes people argue and fight • It takes up too much room so other people can't do what they want to • Some boys don't stop when it's the end of lunchtime • The mud gets brought into school • We can't use rules properly because there's no proper markings	• It's fun for people who enjoy it • When you score a goal you feel good • There's lots of room to play football • You can get better at skills • It's good for your health	• Sometimes it makes me happy, sometimes unhappy • It's cool that we get to play football • I always hope I win • It makes me feel confident • I don't like it because there's not enough room	• We could get a proper pitch marked out so we can follow the rules and don't argue so much • We could have a referee • If we had a softer ball it wouldn't hurt people if it hits them • Part of the field could be marked out so there's room for everyone else as well

Blue hat

When all the points above had been discussed, the children made the following decisions as their preferred solutions:

- Ask the headteacher if we can arrange to have a proper football pitch marked out.
- Find out if someone would be a referee for some lunchtimes – maybe someone's dad would do it.
- Make sure everyone understands the rules.
- Try to remember to clean mud off our boots so the cleaners don't have to clear up after us.

dive below the surface of the story to uncover underlying motivations and purposes, to consider the 'big questions' to which there may be no right or wrong answers. Some examples are shown in Table 7.2.

Using stories for philosophy

When planning to use a story, it is a good idea to prepare some of the questions that could be discussed, but keep them in reserve, as it is better if the children come up with their own suggestions. After reading the story, ask, 'What questions do you have about that story?', or 'What are you wondering about now that you have heard the story?' One way to organise the discussion is to ask the children to write their questions on Post-it notes, which are immediately displayed on the wall. After a few minutes, stop, then, with the class, group the questions into similar topics. Inevitably there will be some simple, literal questions that perhaps others in the class may be able to answer straight away, but you should focus on the more philosophical ones – those to which there is no definitive answer, which are likely to prompt debate. Select perhaps two or three, and either choose one for

Table 7.2 *Stories for philosophy*

Story	Author	Possible philosophy question
David and Goliath	Old Testament Bible story	Can it ever be right to fight and kill?
Rose Blanche	Ian McEwan and Roberto Innocenti	Is war ever a good thing?
Not Now, Bernard	David McKee	Should parents always believe everything their children tell them, and vice versa?
King Midas	Aesop's fable	What makes someone greedy?
Zoo	Anthony Browne	Should animals be kept in captivity?
Little Beaver and the Echo	Amy MacDonald and Sarah Fox-Davies	What is real friendship? Can animals ever be friends?
Can't You Sleep, Little Bear?	Martin Waddell and Barbara Firth	What makes us afraid of things that cannot do us harm?
Farmer Duck	Martin Waddell and Helen Oxenbury	Is it right for one person to tell others what to do? Is revenge ever a good thing?

a whole-class discussion, or ask the children to select one that they will discuss with a partner or small group before feeding back their thoughts to the whole class for further discussion.

Alison read the book *George and Sylvia* by Michael Coleman and Tim Warnes to her Year 2 class. It tells the story of two gorillas who are secretly in love with each other, but each thinks that their size and shape will mean the object of their desire will not love them. Alison had planned questions such as 'Is it right to change yourself so that other people will like you?' and 'Should we all be content to be the way we are whatever others may think or say?' However, because she first asked the children what they were wondering about the story, the lesson took a different direction, as they came up with 'Do animals fall in love?', 'How do we know when we're in love?' and 'What is love?', which had more relevance for the children as they had selected the questions themselves, and arguably were more difficult and more interesting than those that Alison had planned.

Another approach is to ask the children to *draw* what they think are the most important or interesting parts of the story, and to use these as a basis for discussion. Figure 7.4 shows an example of a child's drawing from a Year 2 class who had heard the traditional story of The Goose That Laid the Golden Eggs. Cameron's bold, powerful drawing clearly shows the central role played by the goose. We see the village on the hill behind her, the 'stony path' in front, along which is walking the less important figure (for Cameron) of the man who was given the goose. He was able to use this visual prompt to express his views on the story.

Thinking hard is difficult, but do not be tempted to jump in and help the children answer the questions by giving them clues. Don't be afraid of 'thinking silences'. If we are too concerned with fast-paced lessons, valuable thinking can be lost. We want our children to learn how to think for themselves in order to solve problems and make decisions about how to move forward. Providing the answers for them will not do this.

In order to address philosophical questions, children have to use many different thinking skills, which can be developed through games and activities designed to focus

Figure 7.4 Cameron's drawing of the Golden Goose, following a philosophy lesson

on one aspect of thinking. For example, in order to develop the skills of giving reasons, and justifying choices, children can play the game 'Real or Not Real', based on one of the '20 thinking tools' (Cam, 2006) developed by Phil Cam at the University of New South Wales, Australia, and adapted here:

1. Prepare a set of laminated cards, each with the name of something that could be considered to be real or not real, such as fairies, ghosts, rainbows, dreams, imaginary friends, Winnie-the-Pooh, wishes, Heaven.

2. Seat the children in a circle and place two large cards at either end of an imaginary line on the floor, one saying 'Real' and one saying 'Not Real'.
3. Give pairs or small groups of children one of the small cards for them to discuss whether they think their item is real or not real. Stress that there are no right or wrong answers, but children will have to say why they made their decisions.
4. After a few minutes, those who have been able to agree place their card near the Real card or the Not Real card, showing their decision. Those who have not been able to agree place their cards in the middle.
5. Each pair or group now has to say why they arrived at their decision, by using the word 'because'.
6. Write the headings 'Real' and 'Not Real' on the board or flip chart, to compile a list of the children's reasons.

When Tom did this, some of the responses he got were:

'Things are real if you can see them.'
'Things are not real if you just make them up.'
'Things can be real, even if you are the only person to see them.'
'Things can be real if they have not happened yet.'
'Things are real if you have photographs of them.'
'Things are not real if they are pretend.'
'Things are real if you believe in them.'

These statements are now opened up for discussion and interpretation. It is particularly interesting to discuss opposing points of view, or where comparisons can be made. For example, the children discussing fairies may have agreed that they were not real because they had not seen any, but the pair discussing heaven had agreed that it was real because they believed in it, even though they could not see it. This raises a further question for the class to discuss: do we have to be able to see something in order to believe in it, or to make it real? A good conclusion can be to ask if anyone has changed their minds following the discussions. If they have, ask why, so that they are encouraged to think even further.

A similar activity can be used to discuss whether statements given to the children are 'Fair' or 'Unfair', using real or fictitious situations; or 'True' or 'False' statements such as 'Brothers and sisters always argue', or 'Everybody enjoys Christmas'.

It is a good idea to give the children special books in which to record their thinking and the outcomes of it. Try to build into your philosophy sessions a five- or ten-minute slot at the end where the children can record what they found interesting about the session, what they agreed or disagreed with, something they thought they did well in the session or something they wanted to say but didn't get the chance to.

Mind maps

The technique of brainstorming ideas and recording in a topic web has been familiar to primary education at least since the 1960s. In recent years, the concept has been extended and renamed in the context of speed-reading Mind Maps® by Tony Buzan. While many teachers have used topic webs as a method for planning, it is only recently that it has been introduced to children. It is particularly useful for supporting learning through visual techniques as it uses a combination of colour, symbols, pictures and words. The format of a mind map allows thoughts and ideas to be added to as thinking develops, thus providing opportunities for 'slow thinking' and the development of ideas over a longer period of time.

Essentially, a mind map records in a systematic way all the possible avenues resulting from an initial single idea. Children will need to be taught how to use this technique, but, once learned, it is a tool they can use in any area of the curriculum, and is particularly useful for thinking in a cross-curricular way. Even very young children can be introduced to the technique. For example, many early years and Key Stage 1 classes use the theme of 'Bears' to plan a unit of work because there are many books that use bears as the main characters, and children, of course, love teddy bears. Here's how a mind map might be developed (you can see a teacher's example in Figure 7.5):

1. Get the children to help you construct a mind map by placing the word 'Bears', or a picture of a bear, at the centre of a large sheet of paper, and asking the children to help you to record what we already know, and what we might want to find out (you are including yourself here, of course).
2. Provide some headings to guide the children's thinking. Three headings is probably enough for this age range. With older children, more headings would be used. To help beginner readers or EAL (English as an additional language) children, and to reinforce the visual element of the mind map, include pictures or simple symbols alongside the questions.
3. Selecting one of the headings at a time, think about each more closely and, using the appropriate colour, record the children's responses, discussing where appropriate. Then try to find two or three examples or questions for each of the subheadings.

Figure 7.5 recorded the class's initial thinking about the topic. It could then be used in a variety of ways, for example by inspiring the search for answers to the children's questions, and the production of books and a variety of artwork. The mind map could be displayed as part of a working wall, to which both you and the children can refer as the topic develops, adding extra information as it is discovered. Once children are introduced to this concept, they can begin to use it for themselves as a way of recording their thinking, for example as a form of planning for fiction or non-fiction writing, as part of philosophy, or considering what they know, and need or want to know, in relation to scientific, historic or geographically based themes.

Observation as a basis for developing thinking

By encouraging children to look critically, with a purpose other than to reproduce or remember, you can enable increased interaction, and encourage new areas of thought. This can lead to the possibility of the children creating images of their own relating to the thinking. Here are some example ways of working:

1. Show the children an image of your choice on the interactive whiteboard – a painting or photograph of a scene, a building, a person or group of people – many images are possible. You could also choose a short film clip. If you do, view it with the sound turned off, as it is the visual image that is being considered. Useful websites for accessing photographic images are:

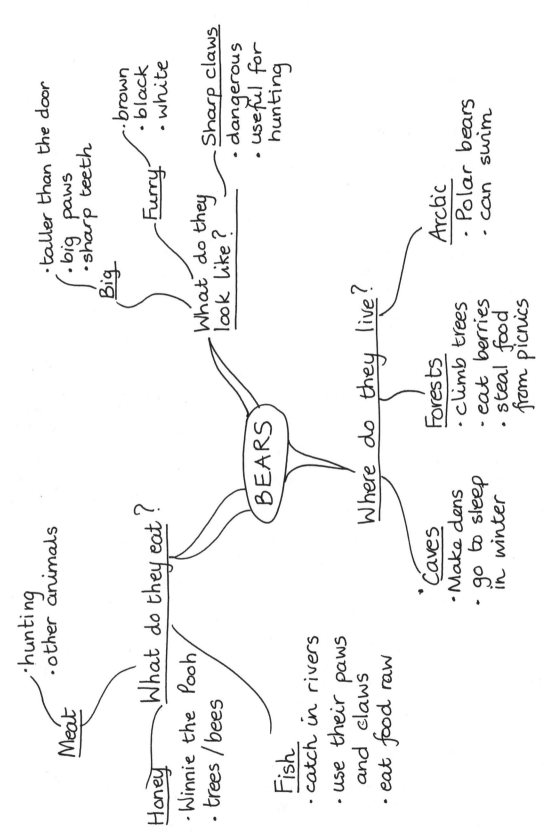

Figure 7.5 Bears mind map

- www.english-heritage.org.uk. Their 'Viewfinder' archive has more than 20,000 searchable photographs.
- www.learningcurve.gov.uk/focuson/film. Here you will find hundreds of short film clips, including early black-and-white documentary clips.

2. Ask the children what the image makes them think about. Is it more than one thing? Is it the same for everybody in the class? Why might it provoke different thoughts? Try to draw out the fact that as we each have a variety of life experiences, so we are likely to react in slightly different ways to all sorts of things, including visual images.

3. Ask the children to note what is there, and also what has been left out. Make the point that the artist or photographer has deliberately selected to frame his image, which involves deciding on what not to show just as much as what to include.

4. Using the original image, or a new one, ask the children whether they think the artist or photographer was trying to make us think of something in particular, or in a certain way. For example, were they trying to make us think of a character as evil, or unhappy; powerful or downtrodden? Were they trying to evoke feelings of wonder, horror, fear or elation? How did they do this? Was it to do with facial expression, body positions, settings, the use of light or colour?

5. Next, give groups of children two or more contrasting images to look at, and ask them to record their thoughts about each one, and also to make comparisons between the two. Once complete, put two groups together to share their observations.

These activities can be repeated several times with a wide variety of images, both still and moving, from a variety of times and cultures. Objects, or photographs of them, could also be used in the same way. What would a pair of iron handcuffs make us think, for example? Or an Egyptian mummy? How about a tobacco pipe? Does it make a difference what setting the object is in? Does our thinking change if we see the object in a different context? You could show the children examples of works by surrealist painters such as René Magritte or Salvador Dali, who challenged conventional thinking through their images. What do they think about the repeated images of Andy Warhol, or the three-dimensional works by Tracey Emin or Damien Hirst? What are they trying to make us think, or think about?

When you feel the children are ready, follow up this exploratory thinking with a task: ask them to plan to take a photograph that is designed to make others think in a certain way. They may want us to think about friendship, our relationship to animals, families, anger, or the future of the planet. They might want us to make a comparison between two things. They may or may not include a person or people in their photograph. They need to think about what to include and what to leave out. Backgrounds are important, as are settings.

When all the photographs have been taken, show them to the class on the interactive whiteboard, inviting children to give their responses. Are they thinking what the photographers intended? Are there any unexpected responses?

Using hidden meanings

Further develop this idea by looking at paintings such as Holbein's *The Ambassadors*, or early allegorical or religious paintings, where certain objects are used as symbols, such as lilies representing purity, a skull being symbolic of death, a scientific instrument showing an interest in science, a telescope representing exploration, or a map standing for discovery. If your interactive whiteboard has a 'spotlight' tool, you can use this to focus the children's attention on specific parts of the painting. Can the children work out what various objects in a painting are making us think about the characters or story that forms the main subject? The children's task following this observational thinking is to plan and create either a painting, photograph or noticeboard that contains specifically chosen objects that will present a particular view of one person, either themselves or a real or fictional character. Once completed, the work can be displayed for others to work out who is represented, and whether it has been successful in portraying the person in the way that the artists intended.

Persuasive images

Armed with their knowledge about how images can be produced to make us think in a particular way, the children could go on to consider persuasive images such as those used in advertising or propaganda. How successfully can our thinking be manipulated? What tricks and skills have been used to make us think in particular ways? Classes studying either world war, or elections, could look at posters and advertisements where words and images are linked in such a way as to influence our thinking. This could lead into children producing their own persuasive images.

By developing children's thinking skills, we are giving them an essential life-skill that is truly transferable. Those children who are challenged in their thinking are more likely to formulate their own questions and devise their own solutions. They will be more likely to think in creative and innovative ways that in turn can challenge us. If we want our children to become active learners, developing their thinking is an essential part of their education.

8 Creativity in the primary curriculum

In this book, we have suggested many ideas that we think are likely to enhance children's creativity. The book as a whole represents a vision of the emphasis on creativity that we think should be applied to the primary curriculum in England. We know that as a well-informed and confident teacher, you can help your pupils' creativity and enjoy creative teaching. However, while we remain optimistic that this is possible, and have shown many examples of teachers (including ourselves) doing this, as an afterword we want to remind you that from time to time you have to fight for what you believe in education. The history of curriculum reform shows us that there are determined forces at work, some of which are not as keen on creativity as we are! (See Wyse (2006) and Wyse *et al.* (2008) for reviews of the curriculum, including some history.) So how does the fight begin? You need to critically evaluate curriculum policy so as not to become a passive recipient and deliverer of the curriculum. This is an entirely appropriate professional stance and an attitude that is likely to ultimately bring you more satisfaction and a greater level of knowledge about the issues.

This chapter illustrates some of the things that you might critique in the defence of creativity. But let us begin with an examination of the language used in official documents. The use of the word 'creativity' as part of curriculum documentation is a small but significant measure of the extent of creativity in the formal curriculum (as an aside, perhaps we should ask ourselves how often we say to children, 'That's really creative, well done!'). The National Curriculum documentation for primary schools does not include the word 'creativity' in its values, aims and purposes. In the section that is the general description about the National Curriculum for Key Stages 1 and 2, the only occurrence of the word 'creative' is in the context of thinking skills: '*Creative thinking skills*: These enable pupils to generate and extend ideas, to suggest hypotheses, to apply imagination, and to look for alternative innovative outcomes.'

Another example of the use of the word 'creativity' in the National Curriculum is seen in the guidance for art and design. The guidance note says that 'during key stage two pupils develop their creativity and imagination through more complex activities', but there is no explicit mention of creativity in the programmes of study. Could this lead to art that is more about pastiche of the work of famous artists and not enough encouragement for pupils to develop their own ideas and styles? We are not suggesting that studying the work of famous artists is without value (including sometimes for creativity itself), but we think that creativity needs to be developed in active ways, in this case through pupils' own creative artwork. In another subject, music, there is an explicit requirement for creativity in the programme of study under the heading: 'Creating and developing musical ideas – composing skills', but this is framed by the necessity to develop 'skills' within 'musical structures'. Once again, this is not without value, but there seems to be no formal explicit encouragement for the kind of creativity that begins openly with the pupils' ideas and encourages them to develop these in ways that are personal to them.

At present, it seems that there are some features of the National Curriculum that should enhance the likelihood of creativity, but it is currently not a *fundamental* part of the curriculum.

A glimmer of hope

Many teachers and schools have continued to offer creative opportunities to children during the period since the Education Reform Act 1988, which first established the concept of a national curriculum. However, in general, heavy prescription through the National Curriculum, national strategies, testing, targets and league tables of test results resulted in an impoverished curriculum, which we suggest was unfit for a mature democratic society. Amid this stormy landscape, a lifeline emerged in the unexpected form of another government report. The National Advisory Committee on Creative and Cultural Education (NACCCE) was established in February 1998 to make recommendations on the creative and cultural development of young people through formal and informal education. There were some powerful messages in the report:

> The real effect of the existing distinction between the core and foundation subjects now needs to be carefully assessed in the light of ten years' experience. It appears to have reduced the status of the arts and humanities and their effective impact in the school curriculum.
>
> (National Advisory Committee on Creative and Cultural Education, 1999, p. 75)

As a way of reducing the curriculum content and addressing the neglect of subjects such as music and art, the report recommended, 'In order to achieve parity, the existing distinction between core and foundation subjects should be removed' (ibid., p. 87). Unfortunately, this recommendation was not followed when the revised National Curriculum 2000 was put into place. The NACCCE report seemed to strike a chord with many people in education who were deeply unhappy about the mechanistic and bloated curriculum that had been followed since 1988. However, in spite of overwhelming support for its message, politicians were not quick to act, and it was not until 2003 that a glimmer of hope was to be seen.

Excellence and enjoyment: A strategy for primary schools (Department for Education and Skills (DfES), 2003) subsumed the literacy and numeracy strategies and was the third major national strategy from the period between 1997 and 2003. It came on top of an unprecedented number of government interventions in primary education. In spite of teachers' feelings of 'intervention overload', it was anticipated keenly because of the growing consensus that educational policy in England was too prescriptive and that this was impacting negatively on creativity. It was hoped that fundamental reforms might result in a more appropriate level of professional autonomy for teachers, including the opportunity to teach more creatively with fewer constraints.

The primary strategy document did indeed include words like 'freedom', 'empowerment' and on page 18, for the first time after the executive summary, the word 'creativity':

> 2.11 Some teachers question whether it is possible to exercise their curricular freedom, because of the priority the Government attaches to improving literacy and numeracy. But as OfSTED reports have shown, it is not a question of 'either', 'or'. Raising standards and making learning fun can and do go together. The best primary schools have developed timetables and teaching plans that combine creativity with strong teaching in the basics.
>
> (ibid., p. 18)

It was somewhat unfortunate that the important idea of curricular freedom was lazily equated with 'fun', another important, but different, idea. However, it is true that schools achieved high standards in literacy and numeracy, and managed to foster creativity in spite of government constraints (indeed, there are some who argue that a creative approach is *more* likely to lead to high standards). But there is a more important consideration: was the primary strategy as originally conceived the *best* way to achieve creativity? If not, what would a better curriculum look like? A brief outline of our view on this comes at the end of the chapter.

One of the most beneficial things to emerge following the NACCCE report was the Creative Partnerships initiative. The Department for Culture Media and Sport (DCMS), Department for Education and Skills (DfES) and the Arts Council started funding Creative Partnerships in 2002. This released £110 million to support the development of 'creative learning' in approximately 900 primary and secondary schools in 36 areas of the country. The main aim was to provide schoolchildren across England with the opportunity to develop creativity in learning and to take part in cultural activities of the highest quality. We hope that this kind of valuable creative work will be sustained in years to come.

Control through the objectives model of teaching

In spite of relentless changes to primary education since 1997, several features have persisted and in most cases been intensified. The testing system, the associated target setting, and statutory control of pedagogy are three prominent examples. The other is the organisation of teaching (particularly literacy and mathematics) through frameworks expressed as lists of objectives, and the application of objective-led teaching as a model for all lessons. Kelly (2004) traces the idea of an objective-led model of the curriculum to the beginning of the twentieth century. The advances in science and technology at that time led to the idea that teaching and learning should be defined more scientifically. However, it was not until nearly one hundred years later that this idea began to be enforced. In the 1970s, pressure grew for the curriculum to be more clearly defined, and as part of this, teachers were encouraged to use the objectives model. In 1997, the frameworks for literacy and numeracy were implemented. For the first time, these listed the curriculum as a series of teaching objectives that pupils 'should be taught'. This prescriptive approach to the curriculum, coupled with the statutory assessment and target-setting system, has resulted in the strongest grip on the school curriculum by government in the history of the English education system. The important point here is that there are many ways to organise curricula, and we all have a right to an opinion about this organisation. In fact, if we look to countries that are England's immediate neighbours, we see very different ways of organising curricula in Wales, in Scotland and in Ireland.

Kelly (2004) identifies a number of theoretical problems with the objective model. First, it is a direct threat to the individual freedoms of pupils and teachers to make decisions about their curricula. He also argues that the model is particularly damaging to subjects such as those in the arts, where good teaching encourages personal interpretation, which should not be determined in advance by teaching objectives. As far as the teaching of English is concerned:

> In literature too the whole purpose of introducing pupils to great literary works is lost if it is done from the perspective of intended learning outcomes (Stenhouse, 1970). Again that purpose is to invite the pupil to respond in his or her own way to what he or she is introduced to. To approach a reading of *Hamlet*, for example, in any other way is either to reduce it to an instrumental role, designed to promote an understanding of words, poetic forms, even philosophy, or to attempt to impose one's own moral and aesthetic values, one's own subjective interpretation of the play and response to it on one's pupils. If appreciation of literature or any of the arts means anything at all and has any place in education, it cannot be approached by way of prespecified objectives.
>
> (ibid., p. 61)

Another way to critique objective-led teaching is ask whether there is empirical evidence to back up the claim that it is the most effective kind of teaching (see Wyse (2003) for a review of evidence on this in relation to literacy).

Given that there is a weak theoretical and empirical justification for the objective model that is so forcefully employed, it is difficult not to see this as a means of control over pupils, teachers and educationists exercised by politicians and policy makers. In reviewing the changes to education over the period of the five editions of his influential book on the curriculum, Kelly (2004) shows that this level of political control has undoubtedly increased, has stifled democratic debate about the curriculum and is even beginning to look somewhat sinister.

Interesting times

From about 2005 onwards, there were positive signs of change. A growing number of people and organisations made their voices heard in relation to the damaging effects of aspects such as the statutory testing system. This resulted in reconsideration of the way that children were summatively assessed. Another example of positive movement was the development of a new curriculum for Key Stage 3 by the Qualifications and Curriculum Authority, based on genuine attempts to involve teachers and educationists.

This was steered by charismatic leadership, sometimes having to work against more conservative forces. The result was a curriculum with more flexibility for teachers, and one that we think is more likely to engage pupils.

At the same time as these kinds of promising developments were taking place, the state was strengthening its grip in other areas – for example, in the early years curriculum. The first Curriculum Guidance for the Foundation Stage represented a reasonable compromise between the government's desire to control and the considerable success of early years specialists to ensure that children's rights to an appropriate curriculum were upheld. However, later the guidance was redrafted and changed from non-statutory to become statutory. This guidance, consistent with all other related national guidance, included strict control over the *method* of the teaching of reading, not just the programmes of learning.

We find ourselves in a time when it is unclear which ideas will ultimately triumph. This is an interesting point in time because there seems to be genuine debate taking place. The continuing desire of the state to control is evident, but there are also signs that people are beginning to stand up more strongly for their beliefs.

In December 2007, the children's plan was presented to Parliament. It was a broad-ranging document containing many promising ideas for supporting children. However, our concern in this chapter is the impact on the primary curriculum and in particular the impact on creativity. The children's plan included the requirement to review the primary curriculum. The selection of Sir Jim Rose to lead a 'root and branch review' (Department for Children, Schools and Families, 2007, p. 9) was seen by many as a controversial choice in view of his recommendations on reading contained in the Rose Review on the teaching of early reading of only a year or so earlier, which resulted in a particular approach to the teaching of reading called synthetic phonics effectively being imposed on England's children (Wyse and Goswami, in press; Wyse and Styles, 2007). In defence of limitations in his report on reading, Rose claimed that the remit set by government constrained his ability to fully review relevant research. For this reason, the specific remit that informed Rose's later review of the primary curriculum was particularly important. Early indications of this were contained in the letter from the Secretary of State for Education, Ed Balls, to Rose confirming his appointment. Consistent with the approach by government since 1997, reading, writing and numeracy skills (but with the addition of 'personal skills') were the first area to be explicitly mentioned in the letter. The location and weighting of topics and ideas in official documents is an important indicator of how their significance is viewed. However, the opening emphasis on the basic skills was quickly followed by the aim for a broad and balanced entitlement to learning 'which encourages creativity and inspires in [pupils] a commitment to learning that will last a lifetime'. Later the letter said that 'a key objective of your review is to enable schools to strengthen their focus on raising standards in reading, writing and numeracy'. The balance between ensuring that basic skills are learned and encouraging creativity is a delicate one. An overemphasis on skills can too easily lead to a restricted curriculum, and one that is less likely to foster creativity.

Another concern we had about the letter was the suggestion that there could be more flexibility in other subjects. Could this mean dropping them altogether, as happened when David Blunkett, a previous Secretary of State for Education, suggested the relaxation of National Curriculum requirements for some of the foundation subjects? The tensions that were evident in this letter mirror the tensions that existed between government desire to control the curriculum and multiple oppositional voices in society complaining about the lack of autonomy and creativity in the curriculum that were clearly evident in the Primary National Strategy, which, in our view, failed to achieve its aims.

Having offered a critique of curriculum policy, we now turn to what we would emphasise in a curriculum for creativity. One of the most important things about the curriculum in future is that the model needs to be relevant from the early years up to the end of schooling and should genuinely prepare students for higher education and lifelong learning. Figure 8.1 presents a simple model to represent some of the ideas that we think should be prominent in the curriculum.

A curriculum model that reflects learning and teaching throughout life needs to put the individual's 'self' at the centre. It is the individual person's motivation to learn and their interests that will sustain learning throughout life. A new curriculum will need to encourage teaching that explicitly encourages pupils to find areas of work that motivate them and to pursue these in depth, even at the very earliest stages of education. Children's rights to participate in all matters that affect them should not be an abstract item in the programmes of study for citizenship but a daily reality in their lives. Role play and drama will be a recurrent medium for reflecting on the self and others. Physical development, including health, will be nurtured as part of this focus.

The environment in which learning takes place is vital to sustain the self. In spite of futuristic claims about learning electronically from home, a place called school will still be the main arena for learning, but it should be one that is not a grimy, damp, cold, boomy Victorian building; it should be architecturally inspiring. It should be a place where the crafts of life, such as the preparation and sharing of food and engagement with music, are centre stage. The social interaction provided by the home and community will form an integrated link with the social interaction provided by the school's curriculum. Sights, sounds and exploration of the world, beginning with the immediate surroundings, will form part of the environmental curriculum. Investigations will take place, problems will be solved and things will be made. All of this will be set in the context of active participation in understanding and working towards a sustainable environmental future for the world.

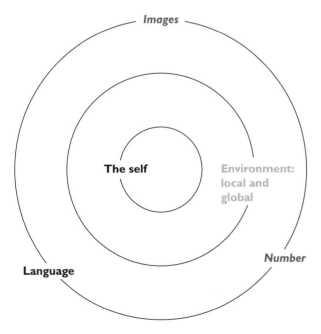

Figure 8.1 Curriculum model

Learning centred on images – both still and moving; icons, logos, signs, symbols – will no longer be neglected in view of the dominant role these things have in our daily lives, and have had for many years. The counting and categorisation of entities, ultimately leading to the beautiful abstraction of mathematical symbols, will remain a powerful focus for learning about number. Language in all its linguistic contexts, including text and talk, will also remain a powerful focus and one that unites all other aspects of this curriculum.

Information technology will not be a subject. Do we have P and P, or paper and pencils, as a subject in the curriculum? No. Information technology will be central to the work of schools, just as any other basic resource is. It will not be used as the latest solution to all our problems, but it will, whenever appropriate, enrich the possibilities for learning and teaching, and its natural influence will continue to grow.

All these areas can and should be part of a creative curriculum. The creative 'self' of the learner will interact with others who encourage creativity. This will happen in the context of creative responses inspired by the senses and communicated through images and text of the widest possible range. Only then, for the first time in history, could the ability to create be *the* fundamental part of the primary curriculum.

References

Amabile, T. (1990). Within you, without you: The social psychology of creativity, and beyond. In M. Runco & R. Albert (eds), *Theories of creativity*. London: Sage.

Banaji, S. and Burn, A. (2006). *The rhetorics of creativity: A review of the literature*. London: Arts Council England.

Booktrust (n.d.). *Writing together: Bringing writers into schools, a practical guide*. London: Booktrust.

Cam, P. (2006). *20 Thinking tools*. Camberwell, Vic., Australia: ACER Press.

Craft, A. (2005). *Creativity in schools: Tensions and dilemmas*. Abingdon: RoutledgeFalmer.

Craft, A., Cremin, T. and Burnard, P. (2008). *Creative learning 3–11 and how we document it*. Stoke-on-Trent: Trentham Books.

Creative Partnerships (2005). *Building creative futures: The story of the Creativity Action Research Awards*. London: Arts Council England and Cape UK.

Creative Partnerships (2008). Home page. Retrieved 18 January 2008 from http://www.creative-partnerships.com/

Csikszentmihályi, M. (1990). The domain of creativity. In M. Runco and R. Albert (eds), *Theories of creativity*. London: Sage.

Department for Children, Schools and Families (2007). *The children's plan: Building brighter futures*. London: The Stationery Office.

Department for Education and Skills (DfES) (2003). *Excellence and enjoyment: A strategy for primary schools*. Nottingham: DfES Publications.

Department for Education and Skills (DfES) (2006). *Learning outside the classroom manifesto*. Nottingham: DfES Publications.

Duffy, B. (2006). *Supporting creativity and imagination in the early years*. Maidenhead: Open University Press.

Feldman, D. H. (2008). Foreword: Documenting creative learning, changing the world. In A. Craft, T. Cremin & P. Burnard (eds), *Creative learning 3–11 and how we document it*. Stoke-on-Trent: Trentham Books.

Feldman, D. H. and Benjamin, A. (2006). Creativity and education: An American retrospective. *Cambridge Journal of Education*, 36(3), 319–336.

Glaser, B. and Strauss, A. (1967). *The discovery of grounded theory: Strategies for qualitative research*. New York: Aldine de Gruyter.

Guilford, J. P. (1987). Creativity research: Past, present and future. In S. G. Isaksen (ed.), *Frontiers of creativity research*. Buffalo, NY: Bearly.

Kelly, A. V. (2004). *The curriculum: Theory and practice* (5th ed.). London: Sage.

Learning through Landscapes (2003). National school grounds survey. Retrieved 1 February 2008, from http://ltl.org.uk/client_files/File/Research/National%20school%20grounds%20survey%202003.pdf

National Advisory Committee on Creative and Cultural Education (NACCCE) (1999). *All our futures: Creativity, culture and education*. Sudbury, Suffolk: DfEE Publications.

Strauss, A. and Corbin, J. (1990). *Basics of qualitative research: Grounded theory procedures and techniques*. London: Sage.

Tranter, P. J. and Malone, K. (2004). Geographies of environmental learning: An exploration of children's use of school grounds. *Children's Geographies*, 2(1), 131–156.

Vernon, P. (1989). The nature–nurture problem in creativity. In J. Glover, R. Ronning and C. Reynolds (eds), *Handbook of creativity*. London: Plenum Press.

Wyse, D. (2003). The national literacy strategy: A critical review of empirical evidence. *British Educational Research Journal*, 29(6), 903–916.

Wyse, D. (2006). Conceptions of the school curriculum. In J. Arthur, T. Grainger and D. Wray (eds), Teaching and learning in the primary school. Abingdon: Routledge.

Wyse, D. (2007). *How to help your child read and write*. London: Pearson Education.

Wyse, D. and Goswami, U. (in press). Synthetic phonics and the teaching of reading. *British Educational Research Journal*.

Wyse, D. and Styles, M. (2007). Synthetic phonics and the teaching of reading: The debate surrounding England's 'Rose Report'. *Literacy*, 47(1), 35–42.

Wyse, D., McCreery, E. and Torrance, H. (2008). *The trajectory and impact of national reform: Curriculum and assessment in English primary schools (Primary Review Research Survey 3/2)*. Cambridge: University of Cambridge Faculty of Education.

Index